The West Indian language issue in British schools

Routledge Education Books

Advisory editor: John Eggleston
*Professor of Education
University of Keele*

The West Indian language issue in British schools

Challenges and responses

V. K. Edwards

Routledge & Kegan Paul
London, Boston and Henley

First published in 1979
by Routledge & Kegan Paul Ltd
39 Store Street, London WC1E 7DD,
Broadway House, Henley-on-Thames, Oxon RG9 1EN and
9 Park Street, Boston, Mass. 02108, USA
Set by Hope Services, Abingdon
and printed in Great Britain by
Lowe & Brydone Ltd
Thetford, Norfolk

British Library Cataloguing in Publication Data
Edwards, Viv
The West Indian language issue in British schools —
(Routledge education books)
1 Minorities — Education — Great Britain
2 Academic achievement   3 Creole dialects,
English — West Indies   4 West Indians in Great
Britain   5 Students — Language
I Title
371.9'7'969729041   LC3736.G6   78-41190

ISBN 0 7100 0172 X
ISBN 0 7100 0173 8 Pbk

Contents

Acknowledgments

Sincere thanks are due to those people who have spent much valuable time reading the original text and suggesting many improvements. These include Rob Jeffcoate, Tim Ottevanger, Anne Roussel, Gwen Smolins, Dave Sutcliffe, Jim Wight, Roberta Wilkins and Howard Williams. I would also like to thank Bob Callaghan, Valerie Glass, Shirley Hadi and Steve Hoyle for their contributions to Chapters 2, 6 and 7; Stephanie Munn for materials on Black Studies; Jean Head for materials on reading; and Sally Fitzwater for her interest and helpful suggestions when typing the manuscript. The staff and children of John Mansfield School, Peterborough, Katesgrove, Newtown and Oxford Road Primary Schools and the Meadway, Westwood Girls' and Alfred Sutton Girls' and Boys' Schools, Reading, have all been extremely co-operative in allowing me to work with them and collect samples of work. And last but not least, I would like to thank my parents, Tom and Hett Edwards, for their truly unselfish help while I was writing this book; my husband, Chris Morriss, for recognizing that women have just as much right to enjoy a career as men and giving me the practical and moral support to do just this; and my son, Dafydd, for understanding that fathers can be just as much fun as mothers during my frequent 'disappearances' to work on the book.

Chapter 1

West Indians in Britain

The background to West Indian immigration

Emigration from the Caribbean to Britain began with the
Second World War, when some seven thousand West Indians
enlisted in the RAF were stationed in the United Kingdom.
Although most went home after the war, high unemployment
there persuaded a considerable number to return. But it was
not only the situation in the West Indies which influenced
their decision to emigrate. All through the 1950s and 1960s
British industry was plagued by a shortage of manpower.
With economic expansion, physically arduous jobs with low
pay and anti-social hours became increasingly less attractive
to the English worker and this created a vacuum which was
filled by immigrant labour. Some employers, including
London Transport and the National Health Service (NHS),
negotiated directly with West Indian governments for the recruitment of skilled personnel, and advertisements for jobs in
England appeared in the press throughout the Caribbean.
Statistics compiled during this period show that peaks in
labour demand were followed by rises in the rate of immigration. It is clear, then, that factors external to the West
Indies were extremely important in population movement.

The precise number of West Indians in Britain is not
known. The influx from the Caribbean remained steady until
the early 1960s, but then rose dramatically with the threat of
immigration control. By 1971 the West Indian population in
Britain was estimated at 543,000, just over 1 per cent of the

1

total population, and this proportion appears to have remained stable. For several years, in fact, there has been no overall immigration from the Caribbean, the number of West Indian-born persons leaving the United Kingdom being greater than that of West Indians entering as immigrants.

The West Indian community in Britain consists of two quite different groups: those who were born and educated in the West Indies, and those who were born or have spent most of their lives in the United Kingdom. Because the West Indian population is, on balance, very young (over half are less than fifteen years of age), this second group is the bigger one. It is, however, neither fully British nor West Indian. Like second-generation Italians or Poles, they have inherited a distinct language and culture, though they rarely identify as strongly as their parents with the country of origin. But whereas an outsider might recognize a Pole or an Italian only by his name, children of West Indian origin are clearly distinguished by their skin colour. There is evidence that, as a result, British society is less welcoming and that this in turn causes young West Indians to identify closely as a group.

It is difficult to know what exactly these young people should be called. This chapter is headed 'West Indians in Britain', but 'West Indian' is hardly appropriate for a group which includes many who have never set foot in the West Indies. 'Children of West Indian origin', 'second-generation West Indians' and 'black Britons' have been suggested by various writers, but none has gained widespread acceptance. A name will no doubt emerge from the West Indian community itself in time, but for the present purpose 'West Indian' is preferred. Although it is recognized that the children we are discussing are British and not West Indian, many of the linguistic and cultural differences which we shall be discussing can be traced directly to their Caribbean heritage. 'West Indian', then, is used as a convenient, if inaccurate, name for this group of children and young people.

The Local Education Authority (LEA) response

Because of the nature of labour demand, immigrant populations are concentrated in conurbations. Greater London and the Midlands have attracted the largest numbers of West Indians, but important settlements are to be found in a number of other centres, including Manchester, Leeds, Nottingham, Bristol, Northampton and Reading. There is a further concentration within these areas and Department of Education and Science (DES) statistics for 1973 show that nearly a thousand schools had over a quarter immigrant pupils. The DES definition of immigrant, however, excluded children whose parents had lived in Britain for ten years or more. The actual concentration of ethnic minority children is thus greater than official statistics suggest.

The influx of immigrant children posed a whole range of difficulties — and challenges — for the education system and is likely to continue to do so for a considerable time. These difficulties were recognized immediately at a grass-roots level but did not receive official recognition until the publication of the DES Statistics of Education for 1970. Since then, a number of researchers have shown that minority-group children's reading standards are lower than those of indigenous children; that they are over-represented in non-selective schools and lower streams and under-represented in selective schools and upper streams (Blair, 1971; Townsend and Brittan, 1972; Little, 1975). Different ethnic groups, however, perform at different levels. This is shown quite clearly by the DES statistics for 1970.

% of	West Indians	Indians	Pakistanis	Non-immigrants
in Educationally sub-normal schools (ESN)	2.33	0.32	0.44	0.68
in selective schools	4	9	9	25
doing non-exam courses	23	26	32	3
doing O levels	6	6	6	42

There appears to be a hierarchical situation whereby non-immigrants do better than immigrants and all immigrants do better than West Indians. Even when ethnic-minority children receive all their education in Britain, their performance is below that of the indigenous population. The figures which

3

produced the greatest protest, however, were those which revealed the over-representation of West Indian children in schools for the educationally sub-normal. On a national level there were proportionately four times as many West Indian children in ESN schools as indigenous children, and in Greater London these figures were higher still.

Collection of educational statistics ceased in 1973. This makes it extremely difficult to monitor the progress of ethnic-minority children, and the DES is considering whether the practice should be reintroduced. As far as we can tell, however, the situation has not changed substantially since 1973. While there are indications that the numbers of West Indians entering ESN schools are decreasing, the overall picture is still very depressing. Evidence given by representatives of the DES to the Select Committee on the West Indian community (HMSO, 1977) indicated that, on average, West Indian children still seem to be performing 'below the level of their indigenous contemporaries'. It was also agreed that 'the phenomenon of low average attainment will not disappear with the virtual ending of immigration from the Caribbean'.

It is interesting to note that despite the disproportion of West Indian underachievers, pupil and parent aspiration remains high. Townsend and Brittan (1972) report that more than twice the proportion of West Indians (69 per cent) as non-immigrants (30 per cent) elected to stay on in school for a fifth year. And even with the raising of the school leaving age, the DES evidence to the Select Committee made it clear that their rate of staying on at school and participation in further education 'compare well with that of indigenous people in similar circumstances'. Bagley's (1975) survey of 2,000 ten-year-old London children showed that Black families are more interested in their children's education than White families; Black mothers read more to their children than White mothers; Black parents are more concerned about their children's homework, and are more likely to have taken them to a library. Low academic achievement clearly cannot be explained in terms of lack of parental support.

The problems of West Indian children have almost certainly been exacerbated by a certain inflexibility in the British education system. This is not to underestimate the magnitude of the difficulties created by sudden influxes of West Indian pupils both for the school and for individual teachers. But, none the less, there seems to have been a reluctance to recognize the special needs of a particular group of children. This can be illustrated, for example, by the assessment procedures adopted for West Indians: while intelligence tests were waived in the case of Asian and European immigrants, they were a normal part of the evaluation of West Indian children. This remained standard practice despite strong evidence that intelligence tests had little validity because of their cultural bias.

There have, admittedly, been attempts to counterbalance cultural differences, but the general consensus is that 'culture fair' tests are implausible and impractical. A series of circulars and memoranda from the DES has stressed that no tests have yet been devised which can be relied upon as the sole instruments for assessing children; and that the best course of action is to observe responses to a stimulating educational environment. But the recognition of the linguistic and cultural differences which put West Indian children at a disadvantage has come very late and has undoubtedly been responsible to some extent both for their wrongful referral to ESN schools and for their over-representation in lower streams.

Factors in underperformance

The main concern of the chapters which follow will be to look at the part which language — and attitudes towards language — may be playing in West Indian underachievement. But it would be unrealistic to think that language can be considered in isolation. There are, of course, many factors which might affect performance and some of the most frequently recurring themes in the debate on the problems of West Indian children are presented below.

Social adjustment

West Indian children arriving in Britain have to make considerable social adjustment. The high cost of travel and the upheaval of setting up home and finding a job lead most parents to leave their children in the care of a relative. As we shall be discussing later in this chapter, the proportion of ethnic-minority members who work in low-status and low-paid jobs is higher than for the population in general, and the median weekly wage of the men is substantially lower than that of White workers. Parents also have to support the children they have left behind, and the financial burden is usually so great that several years pass before they can be reunited. There have been frequent reports of children arriving at the airport who have not known which of the welcoming group was their mother or father.

This, then, is a time of major adjustment for the whole family. Recently arrived children have to come to terms with a new home, a strange country and a very different school system. They obviously miss the West Indies and the people who have been looking after them, and are often jealous of their new brothers and sisters. Children already established in the home also have to cope with feelings of jealousy, and parents, who have made great sacrifices to reunite the family, tend to interpret difficult behaviour on the part of the newcomers as signs of ingratitude.

Children arriving from the Caribbean undoubtedly face special difficulties, but even those born in Britain often start at a great disadvantage. Economic pressures force large numbers of West Indian mothers to work full-time (73 per cent compared with 43 per cent of the general population). There is also a higher-than-average proportion of single-parent families; and the split-shift system, whereby one parent works by day and the other at night, is particularly prevalent in the West Indian community. The chronic shortage of day nurseries and registered childminders, however, means that children are often left in the care of unregistered minders, where the standard of care sometimes leaves a great deal to be desired.

Gregory (1969), in a survey of childminding in Paddington, found that while unregistered minders charged lower fees, they were generally more overcrowded, had fewer housing amenities and took the children out less frequently. Hood *et al.* (1970) report that 53 per cent of the West Indian mothers in their study employed childminders who apparently offered little stimulation for the babies in their care. Pollack (1972b) found that nearly a quarter of the children in her sample had four or more minders in their first three years of life. Inevitably children who have been exposed to this kind of care start school at a greater disadvantage than those who have enjoyed a more stimulating environment. But we should also spare a thought for the mothers of these children. A survey of childminding practices undertaken by the Community Relations Commission (CRC) (1975) draws attention to the degree of worry and anxiety felt by mothers: interviewers received numerous pleas for help and some women were even in tears as they spoke about their children.

Educational expectations

School poses other difficulties. Education in the West Indies is often very different, partly because of material problems and partly because of a different underlying philosophy. The very strict school regime in the West Indies, with its emphasis on rote learning and the 'three R's', is in marked contrast with the more relaxed atmosphere in most British schools. The large numbers of children there (some rural schools have as many as a hundred per class on the register) are only offset by almost institutionalized absenteeism. This means that teachers have to exact very strict discipline in order to make any progress at all.

The dilemma of the West Indian teacher and the consequences for the children she works with are to be seen only too clearly in the reminiscences of a mother born and educated in Jamaica but resident in Leicester since the early 1950s (*Change*, April 1977)

> We children back in the West Indies, we never usually have
> any books to help us and we just can't run to the teacher
> every minute to ask her about what we have to do. We
> have to remember and if you don't, then it's bad for you,
> you will get the strap on your back! I think the teachers
> are really concerned for the children, for them to learn,
> and that's why I think many West Indians are educated
> with the strap.

Education in the West Indies is undoubtedly undergoing rapid change. But the vast majority of West Indians in Britain

7

who received some or all of their education in the Caribbean would have experienced conditions such as these. It must be very difficult, therefore, for West Indian children to reconcile their own preconceptions, or their parents' views on education, with the reality of their very different experience in Britain. They often complain that British teachers are weak, and sometimes they take advantage of this weakness. Teachers, on the other hand, are often bewildered by unruly behaviour at one extreme and withdrawal on the other.

The different value system of the school also has implications for the children's home life. West Indian parents are faced with conflicting ideas as to the most effective way of bringing up their children, since British children tend to be allowed a good deal more latitude than would be acceptable in the West Indies. The situation becomes particularly acute as children reach adolescence, and parents are constantly challenged about their views on education and discipline. This questioning of parental values is not, of course, restricted to West Indian families; but Louden (1977) suggests that the gulf between West Indian parents and children is certainly greater than it would have been in the Caribbean, and it is often far greater than between English parents and children.

Alienation and rejection

The quandary of the West Indian in Britain is difficult to appreciate without a knowledge of the processes of acculturation which he has undergone. Barbados is called 'Little England'; Britain is the 'mother country'; schools have tended to teach British history, geography and literature to the exclusion of anything to do with the Caribbean. Albert Maria Gomes, in an interview with the *Listener*, describes the situation thus (quoted in Rose *et al.*, 1969, p. 437):

> Like every West Indian I am part Englishman. I mean this, of course, in the sense that, having acquired the English language, the traditions and institutions of this country, it is natural for me to want to be here. The West Indian is essentially what British culture and influences have made him.

It is hardly surprising that many West Indians experienced intense pain and rejection when their reception did not live up to expectations.

Employment is an area of particular concern and there is evidence of discrimination in both recruitment and promotion. The 1971 census showed the rate of unemployment to be twice as high among West Indian men and youths as in the rest of the population and even higher among West Indian women. In the period November 1973–5 the total number of unemployed doubled, but the number of minority-group members without work increased four times. And even when West Indians are in regular work, their job levels do not approximate those of the general population. Smith (1976) reports that only 8 per cent of West Indians are in professional and white-collar jobs (compared with 40 per cent of Whites), whereas 32 per cent are in semi- or unskilled jobs (compared with 18 per cent of Whites). More than twice the proportion of minority-group men do shift work and there is a substantial difference between the median weekly wages of the two groups.

It would be wrong, however, to think that this is the only area in which West Indians suffer disadvantage. The ILEA has suggested that West Indian pupils in particular are the victims of multiple deprivation. Using indicators of occupation of head of household (semi- or unskilled workers), poverty (in receipt of school dinners) and large families, they calculated that 16 per cent of West Indian children (compared with 5½ per cent of all the children in their schools) experienced all three forms of disadvantage. Daniel (1968) also points to considerable discrimination in the provision of services and housing. Since West Indians are concentrated in inner-city areas, they share with the indigenous population the problems of overcrowding, sharing and lack of amenities. And one survey (Pollack, 1972b) shows that West Indians pay far more rent than English tenants for far worse housing.

Older West Indians and those who have received only a small part of their education in Britain have tended to seek consolation in religion. The social and cultural role of the Church, and particularly the Pentecostal sects, has often been overlooked; but it has provided a very important focus for a large number of West Indians (reported in Kiev, 1964).

> If I didn't have a church to go to and meet friends, if I
> didn't find someone who understands and speaks the
> language, I'd find it very lonely and very hard in England.
> When you go to church, sing together, read God's words
> together ... might be feeling so sad over conditions, but
> church encourages you.

The importance of the Church extends mainly, however, to older-generation West Indians and children. Among British-born adolescents, many girls attend, but very few boys, and there is a general feeling that the Church promotes what Louden (1977) describes as a 'false and unobtainable value system'. For these young people, their parents' solution is totally unrealistic.

First-generation West Indians were prepared to accept the treatment they received in the hope that their children would be able to play a more equal part in British society. But children are becoming angry that they, too, are expected to fill the same low-status positions. Troyna (1977b) reports increasing disenchantment among the fifteen- to sixteen-year-olds he interviewed in north London and the east Midlands. Michael, for instance, expresses suspicion about employers —

> Some of them are prejudiced. That worries me 'cos when I
> go to get a job and I've got the right certificates for it,
> because I'm not the same colour I'm cheated out of the
> job. I don't like that 'cos I've been cheated.

There is evidence, too, of widespread cynicism and hostility towards statutory employment services. The CRC (1974b) report that approximately half of their sample of young unemployed Blacks were not registered at Careers Offices or Employment Exchanges, presumably because they did not see registration as a means of securing a job.

Unemployment often leads to family tensions, and highlights a whole range of differences of opinions between generations. A young Black interviewed by John (1972) explains:

> Our parents have their own ways of coping in this country
> and we have others. Our methods have got to be different
> because we don't see our situation as our parents see theirs.

Sometimes these differences cannot be resolved and children leave home. This can be the starting point of an unfortunate sequence of events. Homeless, the young Black cannot concentrate on looking for work and without a permanent address it is more difficult to obtain Social Security and Unemployment Benefits. Without money it is virtually impossible to find accommodation. Indications are that only a very small proportion of West Indian youths are caught up in the worst of this vicious circle; but this does not detract from the seriousness of the problem and the very real threat that it poses for young Blacks.

Police/Black relations are another index of alienation. There is widespread mistrust and suspicion of the police; and reports of harassment and brutality in the media and passed along the grape-vine constantly undermine the confidence of the Black community. The police, for their part, complain of undue hostility and paranoia in their dealings with Black people. The situation is aggravated by the high proportion of unemployed youths. Inevitably, they spend more time on the streets, are seen more often by the police and are more likely to be stopped and questioned. The tensions generated have led to what John (1972) has described as a kind of psychological warfare between the two sides; but this psychological warfare is only symptomatic of the increasing gap which is opening up between some Black youths and White society.

One response to this situation is withdrawal into a Black sub-culture which revolves around reggae music and the cult of Rastafarianism. This life-style encompasses only the Black community — the local Black clubs, specialist reggae record shops, shebeens, sound systems and discotheques. As Troyna (1977b) points out, this sub-culture promotes as a positive identity the very Blackness which society in general rejects. It has provided adolescents with a kind of cultural renaissance and has allowed them to develop a greater degree of autonomy from White society.

But feelings of rejection are not restricted to adolescents. Milner's (1975) review of research findings shows clearly that very young children are sensitive to racial difference; and even in the primary school complaints from children that they are being victimized because of their colour are not uncommon. Although acts of blatant discrimination must be rare, it is not difficult to understand why Black children are so sensitive about the treatment which they receive.

A probationary teacher interviewed as part of the Schools' Council/National Foundation for Educational Research (NFER) project on 'Education for a multi-racial society' spoke of the warnings she had received before starting her job about the discipline problems which Black children, and particularly the boys, would cause. Her behaviour in the classroom showed clearly that she had accepted this stereotype and was acting upon it. The Black boys in her class were separated from each other and it was striking that only they, and not the White children, were challenged when they got up from their places. As the lesson progressed it became obvious that the Black boys were responding to this treatment by getting up more often purely for the nuisance value. Hobbs (1976) reports an incident in which a 'dinner-lady', examining the hands of infants for signs of soap and water, took all the White ones in hers but did not touch the Black ones. Examples of this kind may not be frequent, but even one bad experience may have a profound effect on Black children's subsequent reactions to White authority figures.

The implications of insensitivity on the part of the host community to the feelings of young Blacks are far-reaching. As the Community Relations Commission (1974a) points out, there is a real danger that,

> We may produce a lower class, either unemployed or only able to do the most menial work, which will be easily distinguished by colour; a situation which already exists in other countries and one which all those with a concern for good relations in this country would wish to avoid.

Language

Having discussed some of the more important factors which undoubtedly contribute to West Indian underperformance, we can now consider the part which language may well be playing in this process. There has often been a great reluctance to look seriously at this area and, in order to understand why, we need to examine attitudes towards language both in the West Indies and in Britain.

The language spoken by the vast majority of West Indians in the Caribbean is not standard English but a variety variously referred to as 'Creole', 'patois' or 'dialect', very different both in its grammar and its sound system. The language of education in the West Indies is, however, standard English: textbooks are in English and the syllabuses and examinations are, even today, largely geared to the British system. None the less, several writers report that most West Indian teachers habitually use the non-standard forms which they correct in the work of their pupils.

The insistence on the use of standard English is, thus, both impractical and unrealistic. There are reports that as soon as children leave the classroom they revert to and feel more comfortable with Creole. And even in the classroom the teacher has to resort to Creole. Young (1973), a West Indian researcher, writes that three out of four teacher informants admitted using Creole in the classroom because, on the one hand, the children understand better and are livelier and keener to participate and, on the other hand, teachers themselves sometimes cannot express thoughts in English which cause them no difficulty in Creole. One teacher pointed out that when he was in school all comments had to be in 'good English' and that, consequently, many students were so intimidated that they always felt uneasy about speaking in front of the class because of the risk of making mistakes.

Attitudes towards the use of Creole have, thus, tended to be severely critical. Yet they have resulted in very little linguistic change. The 'errors' which have been corrected by generations of teachers continue to be as much a part of West Indian speech as ever. Critical attitudes have produced instead a feeling of inferiority on the part of the majority of the population and great linguistic insecurity on the part of West Indians who have achieved middle-class status and who, as Hymes (1971) suggests, 'loudly proclaim the superiority of their own standard while nursing inward doubts as to whether their English is really sufficient standard'. There have undoubtedly been major steps forward in this area throughout the West Indies, but traditional views towards Creole are so deeply entrenched that the process of change is likely to be a lengthy one.

When one examines the question of Creole in a British

context many similarities emerge. Attitudes towards non-standard speech of all descriptions have tended to be critical and Creole has proved to be no exception. In terms of providing special language-teaching facilities for West Indian children, British schools were either slow to respond or else failed to respond at all. This was often because of an egalitarian philosophy which did not recognize that special needs require special provisions. Many schools were confused as to whether or not West Indians actually had linguistic difficulties, or what action they should take. This either resulted in their ignoring the problem or trying to cope with it on the basis of rather unsatisfactory *ad hoc* arrangements.

Language is a subject about which West Indians tend to be very defensive. Because they have been told repeatedly that Creole is 'broken language' and that those who use it must be very backward, their reaction is often to insist that they speak standard English and deny any knowledge of a distinct West Indian variety. Similarly, the British expect West Indians to speak English – they come, after all, from former British colonies where the offical language is English. And the British reaction when they are confronted with speech which is clearly not standard English is often not favourable. They recognize many of the words as English but the grammar is manifestly non-standard and is often dismissed as 'bad', 'sloppy' or 'inadequate'.

Emotional reactions to West Indian speech have tended to cloud many important issues. Only recently have attempts been made to assess the role which Creole might be playing in inhibiting fluent reading and understanding. It is rare for Creole to be looked upon as a perfectly logical and adequate linguistic system which is the vehicle of a very lively culture. And very few people have considered the harmful effect which constant correcting of Creole features might have on the self-confidence of West Indian children and on their motivation to learn standard English. These are vitally important areas. Although we must not underestimate the part which factors like educational expectation, alienation or social adjustment may be playing in the underperformance of West Indian children, it is essential that we should also look carefully at language. In the early days of immigration it was assumed that linguistic differences would pose a temporary problem, that children would pick up English in the playground. Such a view has been shown to be extremely simplistic, and the situation is such that even second-generation West Indian children can in many cases be shown to be strongly influenced by Creole. It is very important, then, to understand the potential difficulties which language difference may be causing and the role which the teacher plays in the acquisition of British English.

Chapter 2

West Indian Creole

The Creole–standard continuum

The language spoken by almost everyone in the West Indies is generally called 'Creole' by linguists, and 'patois' or 'dialect' by West Indians themselves. The linguistic situation in the West Indies can best be described in terms of a continuum with broad Creole at one end and standard English at the other. Each speaker will command a span of the continuum rather than simply occupying a point on it. Rural, working-class speakers will be nearer the Creole end of the continuum than urban, middle class speakers. Speech is also affected by situation so that more Creole features would be heard in conversations with family and friends than, for instance, in encounters with authority figures like teachers.

It would be misleading, however, to think in terms of separate varieties occurring at different points along the continuum. Bickerton (1975), for instance, uses 'basilect' and 'acrolect' for the broad Creole and standard ends of the continuum and 'mesolect' when referring to intermediate varieties, but there are no definite lines of demarcation between the 'lects', and speakers often shift between broad Creole and more standard speech without ever being aware of this. It is only the preponderance of features from one of the 'lects' which will decide where on the continuum a particular utterance should be placed. The kind of problem which this poses for the linguist can be illustrated by a brief extract from a conversation with a young, Jamaican girl recently arrived in

Britain, in which the italic words represent features of Creole.

> '*Pose* you *baptize*, you see, and you *gwain* to go and *save* God, ... you don't want to go to '*ell to burn up* in the fire, and so you *gwain* to '*eaven* with God, you see. You do the right *ting*, you *baptize* and you repent and talk in tongues.

To the untrained observer switching of this degree would seem to be both unsystematic and motiveless. Close analysis of more extensive stretches of West Indian speech, however, shows that the switching is part of regular, rule-governed behaviour. This can be seen more clearly by examining two short transcriptions of a story told by the same Jamaican girl. The first is intended to be a Creole version; the second is her approximation to standard English. At first sight she seems to show very little variation between the Creole and English accounts, but if we follow one feature – the Creole use of /t/ and /d/ for English /θ/ and /δ/ (as in thin and then) – an interesting pattern emerges.

Creole

Once upon a time, Miss Annancy and Brother Annancy go buy pork. When Miss Annancy go buy *de* pork and come back and come se Miss Annancy sit down. So *d*en Miss Annancy go back and carry pork come put down, Miss Annancy come come, take you time, 'cos for fry it. And when she go in her ba*t*room go bed first, when him done Miss Annancy come and *d*en him come in upon him and cut off him bottom and put it in a pot for fry. And him go back and come back and come back and do *de* same *t*ing.

'English'

Once upon a time Miss Annancy and Bro*d*er Annancy go and buy a pork. Miss Annancy sit down and wait till him come back. When Miss Annancy come come put down *de* pork, she sit down and then Miss Annancy go back and come back and she go in her bathroom go bed and then Miss Annancy come in her ba*t*room and all and cut off her bottom and put it into the pot to fry and then go back and come back and do the same thing.

We find the following pattern:

	t, d	th
'English'	3	6
Creole	6	1

It is clear, then, that there are not two mutually exclusive systems at work but that /t,d/ are more likely to occur in Creole and /θ,ð/ in 'English'. It is not possible to predict categorically when a West Indian will choose one or the other, but this does not detract from the rule-governed nature of their behaviour. Variation of this kind is not, of course, peculiar to Creole but is found in all languages and dialects and corresponds to differences in style and formality.

The historical development of Creole

We have seen in the preceding section that a considerable amount of variation exists in the speech of individuals. But there is also variation from one island to another, and in order to understand the kind of differences which occur we need to examine the historical factors which have given rise to Creole. The French, Spanish, Dutch and English all have colonized different territories; some territories have changed hands several times. There has also been considerable East Indian influence in some parts of the Caribbean, notably in Trinidad, Surinam and Guyana. The linguistic influences which have affected the islands have thus differed from time to time and island to island. One writer, Alleyne (1971), has suggested that starting with Sarammacan, spoken by the Bush Negroes in Surinam, and ending with Barbadian English, a scale of decreasing African speech habits might be constructed. It would appear, then, that we must take into account not only the continuum which is held to exist within a single community, but also the continuum from one island to another.

It is commonly assumed that the largest ethnic group — the African slaves — developed a kind of pidgin English to communicate with their White masters. A more immediate concern, however, was communication among the slaves themselves, since they spoke a wide variety of African languages. The only individuals who had any degree of contact with the European population were the freedmen and artisans, and documents from this period indicate that these particular Africans spoke good, easily intelligible English. Thus the argument that a pidgin was developed for communication between slaves, rather than between slaves and masters, is very convincing.

The extent of linguistic diversity in the early days can be illustrated by a description of Jamaica in the mid-eighteenth century. There were speakers of Creole 'Negro English' who had been settled on the island for some time; newly imported Black slaves speaking various African languages; 'coloured' freedmen and poor Whites who would have spoken a variety of English nearer to standard English; recently arrived indentured servants speaking regional dialects of English; planters and merchants who spoke English with a 'Jamaican accent', and, finally, expatriates speaking upper-class English. Obviously the situation varied from island to island, but this gives some indication of the influences at work.

The early arrivals would have developed a kind of pidgin. The grammar and vocabulary would have been greatly reduced and its range of usage rather limited. But as it became more widely used it would gradually have replaced the native African languages. Parents would have started using it to their children who would have grown up speaking it as their first language. The grammar and vocabulary would have been greatly expanded and we would now be dealing in terms of a creole rather than a pidgin. Where it is possible to argue that pidgins are inadequate linguistic systems, creoles are fully developed languages, capable of expressing the whole range of communicative needs of a population. They are logical and regular and it would be quite wrong to consider them in any way 'broken' or 'inferior'.

Language or dialect

Although Creole shares a large part of the vocabulary of English, it is very different both in grammar and in sound

19

system, and there has been a great deal of disagreement over the years as to whether it should be considered a separate language or simply a dialect of English. Some writers feel that the differences between standard English and Creole are sufficiently great for it to be treated as a separate language. Other writers, however, prefer to think of it as a dialect of English. They consider that the amount of variation which exists in Creole is such that it would be unrealistic to attempt to separate it from English. It can be argued that a certain amount of variation exists within any language, and that the 'switching' between language which occurs, say, in the speech of some French-English bilinguals, is no greater than that found in West Indian speech. But — ironically, perhaps — the decision as to whether a particular linguistic variety is a language or a dialect lies with politicians and not with linguists.

In Scandinavia we find a dialect continuum from Norway in the north through Sweden to Denmark in the south. People who live at neighbouring points on the continuum have no difficulty in understanding one another, though communication between Norwegians at the northern extreme and Danes at the southern extreme would be very difficult. The separate political development of the three countries has, however, resulted in different national norms and different standard languages. On the other hand, the differences between classical Arabic and the local 'dialects' spoken in the various Arab countries are often far greater than those held to delimit separate languages in Scandinavia. In this case, the differences are minimized for cultural reasons, and linguistic unity can be seen as an important instrument in Arab political unity. The definition of language and dialect thus often depends on non-linguistic considerations.

As far as the West Indies are concerned, strong cases can be made both for and against giving Creole the status of a language. Its adoption as the national language would seem an important symbol for developing political consciousness in the Caribbean. It might also mean that it would be used as the medium of education, in the early years at least, and as the discussion in Chapter 1 has made clear, this would be highly desirable. But we also have to take into account the Creole legacy of inferior status. When Le Page, a linguist working in the Caribbean, suggested in the 1950s that Creole should be used in schools, Vere John of the *Kingston Star* considered this to be a 'pernicious and insulting idea'. More recently attempts at curriculum reform in Trinidad and Tobago which recognize Creole as a valid linguistic system have provoked an equally outraged response. None the less, the new nationalist pride among West Indians, together with more liberal views towards Creole, may well prevail in time over more conservative attitudes, so that, politically, the status of Creole remains an open question. Linguistically, however, it should be stressed that the decision is largely irrelevant, in so much as Creole is a perfectly adequate linguistic system, whether it be labelled language or dialect.

A description of Creole

Finding out about Creole is not always an easy matter. One of the problems is that most descriptions deal with Jamaican Creole, and a teacher working in a predominantly Barbadian settlement like Reading, or a predominantly Vincentian settlement like High Wycombe, has no way of knowing how similar — or different — the language of their children is. Another difficulty is that descriptions of Creole tend to be written by linguists for linguists and inevitably become involved in discussions of a technical nature which are of little interest to non-specialists.

Much of the discussion in this book will be directed at the educational implications of Creole and it will be argued that a basic knowledge of the language of West Indian children is essential for the teacher. Without this knowledge, it will not be possible to discriminate between genuine mistakes and features of Creole in the children's work. There may also be a temptation to label their language as a 'broken' form of standard English, instead of recognizing it as a perfectly valid linguistic system in its own right.

It is very important, therefore, that teachers and others working with West Indians should have access to a general account of the main differences between Creole and standard English. Very often these differences are common to all the islands, but some features do vary. Although it would be tedious simply to catalogue the differences, it would be

21

misleading to suggest that all West Indians speak the same variety and so variation will be indicated when it is known to occur.

The various influences on Creole are clearly to be seen. Sometimes there is evidence of African influence both on vocabulary and on grammar. Sometimes there are features, such as lack of inflection, which are common to other pidgins and creoles in many parts of the world. It is interesting to note, however, that where standard English distinctions have been lost, alternative means of expression have nearly always evolved in their place. The fact, therefore, that Creole shares a vocabulary base with English does not detract from the fact that it is often fundamentally different.

It has already been suggested that Creole is no less logical, regular or adequate a linguistic system than standard English, and emphasis will be placed throughout the description on the idea that Creole is different, but not deficient. An attempt will be made to reduce technical terminology to a minimum and to restrict discussion to those areas which are essential for an understanding of the structure of Creole. The account which follows is, therefore, more of an outline than an exhaustive description. Readers interested in a more detailed discussion may wish to consult the works listed in Suggestions for further reading for this chapter.

Creole phonology

The sound system or phonology of Creole is very different from that of British English. There is considerable variation from island to island resulting in the typical Jamaican or Trinidadian or Grenadian accent. But the sound systems of the different islands also have many features in common, and it is these shared features which are of special interest.

Creole has a smaller number of phonemes, or distinctive sounds, than British English in the same way that RP, or the Received Pronunciation associated with BBC newsreaders, has fewer sounds than Welsh English. It also has fewer possibilities of combining these sounds, so that certain clusters of consonants are never found at the end of words. An interesting consequence is that many words which are distinct in British

English are homonyms in Creole. The examples given below will make this clear. The first column shows the RP sounds which interest us; the second column shows the single Creole sound which corresponds to the RP sounds; and in the third column there are examples of the different British English words which are pronounced identically in Creole.

Received Pronunciation	Creole equivalent	Resultant homonyms
/æ,ɔ/	/ a /	rat, rot
/ai,oi /	/ ai/	tie, toy
/ʌ,ɜ·/	/ o /	bud, bird
/ iə,ɛə/	/ ia /	fear, fare
/ʌŋ,aʊn/	/ ong /	tongue, town
/ t,θ/	/ t /	tin, thin
/ d,ð/	/ d /	den, then
at the end of words:		
/n,nd /	/ n /	fine, find
/ l, ld, lt /	/ l /	coal, cold, colt
/k, kt /	/ k /	tack, tact
/ f, ft /	/ f /	laugh, laughed
/s,st,sk /	/ s /	mass, mast, mask

Context will help to resolve many of the ambiguities, in the same way that English speakers have no difficulty in distinguishing between 'meet' and 'meat' or 'see' and 'sea'. There are also certain Creole innovations which reduce the potential number of ambiguities. We have already seen, that RP /æ/ and /o/ are pronounced as /a/ in Creole words like 'pat' and 'pot'. We would therefore expect both 'cat' and 'cot' to be pronounced as /kat/, but it is interesting to find that Creole preserves the difference in a rather novel way. When /k/ and /g/ come before RP /a/, Creole inserts a /y/ sound so that we find

kyat — cat
kat — cot
gyaadn — garden
gaadn — Gordon

Similarly, English 'bile' and 'boil' become Creole /bail/ and /bwail/, the /w/ sound preserving the distinction between the two words.

23

Differences in stress and intonation also contribute to the particular West Indian quality. It is very difficult to discuss intonation, since it requires a training in phonetics to be able to identify the various patterns. We will have to limit our- selves, therefore, to simply pointing out that marked differ- ences occur, creating an effect which most British people label 'sing-song'. Differences in stress, however, are much easier for the untrained observer to identify. Some words are always stressed differently so that, for instance, *dirty*, *orchestra* and *blackberry* are stressed on the first syllable in English and on the second in Creole. And accentuation can even be used to distinguish between words so that in Bar- badian Creole *copy* can be a verb or a noun, and *brother* can be a male sibling or a member of a religious sect, according to the way in which they are stressed.

Creole vocabulary

There are many influences on Creole vocabulary, but English is by far the most important. Quite often, however, Creole and British English have developed in different directions. Thus, some Creole words like 'mell' (annoy) and 'picker' (pickaxe) are now obsolete in British English. Other Creole words retain a sense once common but now obsolete in English, and these include 'child' (a girl friend or lover), 'grudge' (to envy) and 'box' (to strike). There is also a group of words, which includes 'maggich' (maggots) and 'maliflaking' (beating), and can be traced to English dialectal usage. But perhaps the most interesting words are those which have developed a new sense. Thus, 'stain' means 'to taste sour' or 'to be sticky', 'to look for' means 'to visit', 'foot' means the whole leg including the foot.

The East Indian influence can be seen in a small number of words of Hindi origin, such as 'ganja' (hemp) and 'roti' (bread). Similarly, French and Spanish influence is to be found in islands where there has been French or Spanish occupation, or where there has been migration to territories where these languages are spoken. But a more significant influence comes from African languages, and words from a wide range of dif- ferent languages have been identified. This African element is strongest in Jamaican Creole, though other islands show evidence of this influence, too. Thus 'ashum' (from Twi *o-siǎm*) is used in Jamaica, Grenada, Antigua (*ashum*) and Belize (*kaa-sham*) for 'parched and ground corn', and *jook*, 'to pierce' (cf. Fulani *jooka*), is used in Grenada, Trinidad, Barbados and Jamaica.

Creole nouns

The main way in which Creole nouns differ from English nouns is in the formation of plurals. English generally adds an 's', but in Creole the noun is invariable. Compare

> British English: Six boys visit the house every day
> Creole: Six boy visit the house every day

In the English sentence plurality is marked three times: first in the number six; then by the plural suffix 's', and finally in the verb, which would have been 'visits' and not 'visit' in the singular. In the Creole sentence, however, 'six' is the only marker of plurality: 'boy' stays the same, and, as we will see later, the verb is also invariable. In cases such as this, the various markers of plurality are largely redundant; as Creole demonstrates, one marker is sufficient.

But in situations where it is important to show that we are talking about more than one person or thing, Creole has a quite distinct way of marking plurality. In Jamaican Creole, for instance, we find:

> De boy – dem look for her all the time
> (The boys visit her all the time)

An extension of this usage is found in:

> Jane-dem (or Jane an dem) like your brother
> (Jane and her gang like your brother)

A second way in which Creole and English nouns differ is in their treatment of possession. In Creole this is shown by the relative positions of possessor and possessed:

> Armstrong coat
> The girl brother

This, in fact, is an extension of a process which already exists in English neuter nouns. Thus, we say 'the desk drawer' not 'the desk's drawer', and 'factory floor' not 'factory's floor'. But here, too, Creole has developed a quite distinct way of expressing possession: /fi/ or, occasionally, /fo/.

$$\left.\begin{array}{l}\text{Di hat a fi Jan} \\ \text{fi Jan hat}\end{array}\right\} \text{John's hat}$$

Pronouns

This is an area in which there is considerable variation from island to island, though in all cases there is a good deal less inflection than in English. Like English, Creole marks person and number but gender is only marked in some instances and case only for the first person singular, and only in some islands. The table below shows the kind of variation which exists.

	I	you	he, she	we	you	they
Belize	a	yu	i	wi	unu, aal a unu	de (dem)
Jamaica	mi (a)	yu	im (shi)	wi	unu, aal aa unu	dem
Nevis	mi (a)	yu	hi, shi	aa wii	aa yu, yu aal	dem
Antigua	mi	yu	hi, shi	aa wi	aa yu, yu	dem
St Vincent	mi	yu	u, shi	aa wi	aa yu	dem
Barbados	a	yu	hi, shi	wi	yu, yu aal, aa wuna	de (dem)
Grenada	a	yu	hi, shi	wi	amongse-yu, among-yu	de
Guyana	a (mi)	yu	hi, shi	wi	yu aal	dem

Even when English pronouns are found, they do not always correspond to standard usage. Thus, he and she are often used in Creole to express possession, whereas in English we would expect *his* or *her*.

Take she back to she mother
(Take her back to her mother)

The English pronoun system, however, can be seen to be

largely redundant, since word order makes their function in the sentence quite unambiguous. Creole, in any case, is simply reflecting a tendency which already exists in English: for instance, *it* is both nominative and accusative, and *her* is both possessive and accusative.

Creole verbs

Tense, person, number

The Creole verb, like the noun, is invariable: number, tense and person are not marked by inflectional endings as they are in English. This is seen clearly in the Creole treatment of tense.

> John come yesterday
> Winston walk to school last week
> Jane and Mary go back soon

Although Creole does not make use of inflection, meaning is made clear by adverbial expressions of time or by context. There are also verb particles which can be used to show that an action has been completed. In Jamaica, for instance, you can hear a variety of forms including *en, ben* and *wen*; in Belize and Antigua you find *min* and in Barbados *did*.

> He *did* see the teacher – he saw the teacher
> John *en* come here yesterday – John came here yesterday

Although forms like *Mary smiling, the dog barking* are common, it is also possible to show that an action is in progress in a distinctly Creole way. Again, the exact form varies from island to island: in Belize and Nevis this is *da*, in Antigua it is *a* and in Jamaica both *da* and *a* can be heard.

> Adonis *a* eat the food – Adonis is eating the food
> Elmina *da* work hard now – Elmina is working hard now

The characteristic lack of inflection is also to be seen in the Creole treatment of person and number: there is no concord between subject and verb:

> Jane stay here all the time

Uleen and Thelma read the book
Angela start work today

It is interesting to note, however, that the 's' suffix of the third person singular in English is a relic of a more extensive system (thou givest etc.) and is, in fact, largely redundant.

Voice

The treatment of voice in Creole is also quite interesting. Whereas English has two voices — active and passive — there is no passive voice in Creole and this would seem to be a feature which is acquired very late in the English–Creole continuum. The English active form can be used in Creole to express both active and passive English meanings. Sense is usually made clear by context. This is a feature of all the islands:

the factory take down — the factory was taken down
this can't share   — you can't share this
that thing use a lot   — that thing is used a lot

Related to the absence of the passive voice is the Creole use of certain adjective and infinitive constructions. In English these constructions can be divided into two kinds: those which are like 'easy to please' and those like 'eager to please'. Thus, in the English sentence

John is eager to please

John is the instigator of the action: it is he who wishes to please. However, in the sentence

John is easy to please

John is the recipient of the action, and some other person finds it easy to please him. The 'easy to please' pattern is, in fact, limited to a small number of adjectives which include *hard*, *difficult*, *tough* and *simple* and the vast majority of English adjectives follow the same pattern as *eager*. Creole, however, has conflated the two patterns:

He ain't easy to beat up — he doesn't beat people up easily
He's easy to annoy — he annoys other people easily

The different treatment of the passive should in no way be taken to indicate that Creole is inadequate. Few people would suggest that English is inadequate because it does not have the middle voice of Ancient Greek. Besides, meaning is generally made clear by context.

Copulas

The copula is a collective term for the various forms of the verb 'to be' (*is, am, are, were*, etc.) and there are several important differences between Creole and English treatments of this feature. In English the subject is invariably followed by a verb:

John walked home
The man bought a dog

In Creole, however, there are a number of other possibilities. The subject can, for instance, be followed directly by an adjective:

The girl happy
Beverley sad

-ing forms of the verb can also follow immediately after the subject:

Me and my friend *we chewing* gum but when Miss look up we take it out
Beverley coming back soon

With nouns and locatives the situation is a little more complicated. In Broad Creole *a* precedes noun complements while *de* appears in locative clauses. Thus we find

John *a* big boy
Mary *a* di leader
Money no *de* pon mango tree, but mango *de* pon mango tree

It would seem logical to call these particles verbs, but if we do this we will be faced with certain problems when we consider variation along the continuum. Whereas they undoubtedly function as verbs in broad Creole, it becomes more and

29

more difficult to decide how they should be analysed as we approach the standard end of the continuum. Sometimes they are omitted altogether:

That the first thing me want to do

Oh no, no white people live up our part. They in Kingston, but them clear black our part.

Who she?

This means that a wide range of forms appear sometimes without the copula, and

Mary here
Mary the mother
Mary happy
Mary singing

are all possible, under certain circumstances, for West Indian speakers. Similarly, the infinitive form *be* is sometimes omitted:

You must happy
It won't long

Other features of the Creole verb

Three other features of the Creole verb, all markedly different from English, deserve special mention. The first concerns the Creole tendency to string verbs together without any connecting words. The effect produced is very 'un-English':

When I came to this country I saw old people, especially in winter, *running, going hastling* to catch a bus to work.

So then Annancy *go back and carry* pork *come come put down.*

The second feature concerns a group of verbs which relate to the psychic state of the subject. The most common of these verbs are *tell, know, mean* and *hear* and they are followed by the particle /se/. This functions very much like a relative pronoun, but is more likely to derive from West African Akan *se*, which introduces the words actually spoken, than from English *say*:

30

He told me se, well we haven't got any vacancy right now and the gentleman asks for I like to go elsewhere. He told mc se well alright, you go back.

Finally sentence structure may vary considerably in Creole and the way in which clauses are joined is often very different:

I have a brother if he was here he help you
(I have a brother who would help you if he were here)

What the difference bctween I read this newspaper or this book?
(What's the difference between me reading this newspaper and this book?)

A run John run make him fall down
(It's because John ran that he fell down)

Creole morphology

Whereas grammar deals with the relationship between words, morphology deals with relationships within the word. English morphology can be divided into two main categories for the purpose of comparison with Creole: suffixing structural pointers and grammatical suffixes. Grammatical suffixes like -*s* of thc plural and -*ed* of the past tense have already been discussed in the sections on nouns and verbs. This leaves us then with the suffixing structural pointers.

There are a number of suffixes in English which show the part of speech to which a particular word belongs. A comparison with Creole, however, shows that quite often the same suffixes are used to designate different parts of speech. The -*ify* suffix, for instance, is only attached to verbs such as *horrify* and *rectify* in English. But in Creole it appears in words like *jokify* (jolly), *heatify* (hot), *boasify* (proud) and *fussify* (fussy). The -*y* suffix usually associated with English adjectives like *happy* and *sleepy* is found in Creole *greedy* (greed), *cheeky* (to cheek) and *ready* (to get ready). Similarly, the -*ly* suffix most commonly associated with adverbs in English has been reported in Creole *softly* (soft) and *casually* (casual).

The situation is complicated still further by the fact that

31

quite common English words operate as different parts of speech in Creole:

> She going to give him a terrible *punish*
> Stealing and *kill* is the worst thing
> I don't *custom* to use bad word

Mention must also be made of morphological devices peculiar to Creole. It is possible to form demonstratives, for instance, by adding *de* and *ya* to the noun:

> da book—de – that book
> da book—ya – this book

Reduplication is another feature of Creole. This is an iterative device which has a wide range of uses. It can express repetition as in *beat-beat* or *kill-kill*. It can express continuation as in *look-look* or *talk-talk*. It can also communicate the idea of abundance: *bit-bit* (many bits), *wasp-wasp* (lots of wasps); or of distribution: *one-one* (one by one), *little-little* (little by little). Another possibility is intensification so that *pretty-pretty* comes to mean 'very pretty indeed' and *fast-fast* means 'extremely fast'.

One final feature can be mentioned conveniently at this point. There is a very strong tendency in Creole to make use not only of reduplication but also of repetition, especially in story telling.

> All at once de plane going along, for ever going up,
> for ever going up, for ever going up, up, up, up, up, up,
> straight up like a eagle hand, up, up, up, yonder, up, up, up,
> so, yonder like eagle start going up, then I feel it, you
> could tell when it change the going up position.

Negation and interrogation

Creole patterns of negation and interrogation are quite distinct from standard English. Negation, however, is treated in a similar way to many non-standard varieties of English and there are several possible combinations of negative elements:

> (a) Me no call you already? – Haven't I called you already?

   (b) No climb no tree because perhaps you will fall off —
      Don't climb trees in case you fall off
   (c) Nobody no cook no food for you — Nobody is cooking
      any food for you

This kind of negation is usually called double negation, though, as example (c) clearly shows, it is more properly known as multiple negation. It is one of the most socially stigmatized of all non-standard features and often meets with overt disapproval from standard speakers. Usually the 'two negatives make a positive' argument is invoked, which seems to beg the question: languages are full of irregularities and redundancies and it is difficult to see how mathematical principles can be applied to discussions about the way people speak. There are also inconsistencies in this argument. Presumably, since two negatives are held to make a positive, then three negatives will make a negative, which is precisely the case in example (c). Standard speakers, however, would object just as strenuously to 'Nobody ain't got none' as to 'I ain't got none'. It seems illogical, too, to decide that non-standard varieties of English should be stigmatized for their use of multiple negation when many other languages express negation in the same way without any note of censure. Nobody suggests, for instance, that the French speaker who says 'Je n'ai rien vu' really means 'I have seen something'.

    Interrogation in Creole, however, bears little relationship to non-standard English varieties. Whereas both standard and non-standard English usually invert word order to form questions, Creole retains declarative word order and uses interrogative intonation:

    What you want me for?
    Me have money tree 'pon me?
    Who tell you that?
    Where me fi get it from?
    How much you want?

This, in fact, is a feature which is characteristic of even the standard end of the continuum, and questions like

    What time it is?

are quite acceptable even from high status speakers in formal contexts. It is interesting to note that although this is an important difference from the standard it is a pattern reminiscent of Spanish and less formal varieties of French — ¿*ha comido?*; *c'est vrai?* It is also, of course, a pattern common to many pidgins and creoles.

The language of young West Indians in Britain

So far our discussion has revolved around language use in the West Indies. To what extent, however, are West Indians born in Britain influenced by the language of their parents and older members of the West Indian community in this country? In their evidence to the Select Committee on Race Relations, the Community Relations Commission claimed that most children of West Indian origin spoke the same way as their peers; and that the language problems of West Indian children are concerned with general language development and are not specifically related to dialect. Wight (1976) makes the same point:

> Nearly all those West Indian children whose parents speak a broad West Indian dialect are bidialectal. They will speak one dialect with their family and other West Indians, another with their white peers (and perhaps a third with their teacher).

Claims of this kind, however, are seldom well documented; they tend to be anecdotal and impressionistic and there is, in fact, a growing body of research which suggests quite different conclusions.

The most informative study produced to date on the language of West Indians in Britain is that of Sutcliffe (1978). In careful analysis of tape recordings of thirty-two West Indian secondary school children in Bedford, of whom sixteen were born in this country, he found only one to have phonology and grammar identical to the local white norm. In the area of phonology he found that many of the vowel sounds that act as class markers in British English tended to be neutralized by West Indians even in their most 'English' speech. For instance, RP /i:/ and /u:/ (as in 'feed' and 'room') tend to be pronounced as diphthongs /əɪ/ and /əu/ in Bedford and other south-east English dialects. West Indians, however, favour the

RP pronunciation. They also tend to use /h/ more often, and intervocalic glottal stops ('bo'le' for 'bottle') are very much less common. Other features of working-class phonology have, however, been assimilated. Black and White speakers tend to use /v/ and /f/ for /θ/ and /ð/ in words like 'bathe' and 'teeth'; and both prefer /in/ for /iŋ/ in verb forms and participles like *'walking'*.

There are also grammatical differences, and certain Creole forms persist in the speech of very many West Indians, even those born in Britain. These include invariant forms for plural nouns, the third person singular and past tense (*two dog; he see; he go home yesterday*); and zero copulas, particularly before adjectives (*they happy*). There is also a range of features not commonly identified with West Indian speech, some of which persist in even the most English part of the continuum. These include the 'quote' verb *se* and certain aspects of sentence structure. The Sutcliffe data contain examples like:

> So I just knocked him out of bed and jumped in, and then he turn on the light again *se* boy what are you doing there?
>
> Them boys, when they came in they stepped on my bag and all my sandwiches broke up.

The second example is particularly interesting. Sentence structure follows the Creole pattern whereby temporal clauses and adverbs are placed between the subject and verb of the main or embedded clause; 'broke up' is preferred to 'squashed'; and there is evidence of the Creole dislike for passives. Yet, this statement is fully inflected and contains none of the features usually associated with West Indian speech. It is not difficult to understand when we consider examples such as these why teachers and others should feel that West Indians speak like their White peers, for unless they have an intimate knowledge of Creole they are unlikely to detect its influence on the way many West Indians speak. Sutcliffe has called this phenomenon 'camouflaged Creole' and has drawn our attention to an extremely important area.

The picture which some writers draw of West Indian children as bidialectal is clearly an oversimplification. It would be quite wrong to imagine that all West Indians speak two or more quite distinct dialects, each of which is reserved for a

35

particular context. What takes place is a gradual shift whereby the child in the relaxed atmosphere of conversation with peers may use significantly more Creole features than in a formal situation such as an interview with a teacher or headmaster. The incidence of Creole features depends, of course, not only on situation but on the individual concerned. Some West Indians – though the Sutcliffe data indicate that their number is small – will have no Creole features at all in formal situations; others will have speech which is recognizably West Indian even in the most formal situations. But the fact that we are dealing with a continuum rather than a number of discrete varieties means that there is constant interplay or 'interference' between different parts of the continuum.

Wight claims that in their formal speech and writing in school West Indians opt overwhelmingly for British English grammatical forms and that this indicates considerable control over standard English. This seems, however, to beg the question. Sutcliffe's data on the speech of West Indians and the analysis of written work in Chapter 4 show extensive evidence of interference from Creole at all levels. The idea that most West Indians are bidialectal, i.e. that they have total control of two different dialect systems, is, to say the least, contentious.

Evidence from tests designed by the present writer to assess the degree of dialect interference throws further doubt on the notion that widespread bidialectalism has already been achieved (Edwards, 1978b). Differences between West Indians recently arrived from the Caribbean and those who received all or most of their education in this country tended to be superficial. There was evidence of Creole interference in all the subjects tested, including those born in Britain. The question which remains to be asked, however, is at what point dialect interference starts to pose educational problems for West Indian children; and this is a question which we will be considering in greater detail later in the book.

Who speaks Creole, when and to whom?

The extent of Creole usage and the circumstances under which it is used constitute another area which has been poorly researched and little understood. It is commonly assumed that there is a dichotomy of usage whereby Creole is reserved for the home and English for school. The small amount of information available, however, suggests that this represents a considerable oversimplification. Sutcliffe (1978) administered a questionnaire in structured group interviews to forty-seven British- and Caribbean-born West Indians. His subjects reported the following patterns of language use:

Low use of Creole	_High use of Creole_
to siblings	from parents
to parents	to peers

Recordings in a wide range of settings substantiate these claims. Only two of the sample claimed that they used no Creole at all, while 88 per cent of the Caribbean- and 79 per cent of the British-born subjects admitted speaking Creole of a broadness equivalent to

me asks di man fi put me money eena him pockit

It should be mentioned at this point that self-evaluations of language use are notoriously unreliable. Labov (1966), for instance, notes that his informants regularly claimed to use prestige forms, whereas recordings of their actual speech showed that this was not the case. Given the low status of Creole and the fact that many West Indians will only admit to using 'English', it is surprising that a questionnaire should reveal such widespread acknowledgment of the use of Creole. The group situations no doubt contributed to the frank responses, but otherwise the results reported by Sutcliffe can only be attributed to his ability to communicate his positive feelings about Creole.

Similar results were also achieved by Hadi, who used a modified form of the Sutcliffe questionnaire in a project with first-year children in a multiracial comprehensive school in the Midlands. Sixteen out of twenty-two West Indians said that they sometimes used Creole of a broadness equivalent to 'me asks di man ...'. Although answers to a question about who spoke most Creole at home were not as conclusive as in the Sutcliffe research, there was general agreement that Creole was used widely to their friends at school and was often triggered by stress — anger, excitement, joy, playing cards, 'when there is a fight' or 'someone shout at me'.

Their reactions to questions on the use of standard English were also interesting. They were asked what friends would think if they spoke in the standard — would they be considered (a) posh, (b) imitating someone for fun or (c) nice to listen to? British children tended to think they would be regarded as posh rather than mimics, underlining the class boundaries which accent delineates. With West Indian children, however, the situation was reversed and more thought that they would be believed to be imitating someone. Some added that they would be accused of showing off, being English or being mad. This seems to indicate that West Indians very often consider the standard as alien and that they would depersonalize themselves if they were to use it with their friends.

Creole thus appears to be used widely by both Caribbean- and British-born West Indians and in many cases it is likely to influence both the production and comprehension of standard English. There is, however, great sensitivity as to when and to whom speech from the Creole end of the continuum should be used and there is considerable linguistic adjustment from one situation to another. There is certainly no justification for the opinion often voiced by some teachers that West Indians do not know when to use standard English. A study of the whole range of a child's speech shows considerable flexibility and versatility. Nor should it be in any way surprising that Creole is widely spoken amongst second-generation West Indians. The attitude towards children from different linguistic backgrounds has always been that they will 'pick it up in the playground'. Experience has shown that this is not the case, and there are many reasons why this should be, not least when we consider the situation of the West Indian child. Because accent and dialect mark us as belonging to a particular group with particular values, the only way in which we can be persuaded to change the way we speak is because we want to identify with members of another group. The motivation of West Indian children to identify with speakers of standard English and, to a lesser extent, with speakers of regional British dialects, is low. Their feelings of alienation and rejection have already been discussed in Chapter 1. The urgency for young Black Britons to establish their own separate identity cannot be overestimated and one of the ways in which this identity can be manifested is in their speech.

Reports from various sources indicate that this is a rapidly growing phenomenon. Teachers often remark on how a child whose speech in primary school was not noticeably West Indian becomes markedly more so in the course of his time in secondary school. And parents from islands like Barbados and St Vincent can often be heard to comment that their children 'sound Jamaican'. Jamaicans form 60 per cent of the West Indian population in Britain and it seems as if Jamaican English is becoming the most dominant linguistic force in the lives of many Black youths.

The influence of Jamaica is also to be seen in the popularity of reggae music. Troyna (1978) reports that Black pupils in lower streams tend to belong to racially exclusive peer groups and that this would seem to result from their realization of 'a common identity and shared destiny'. This racial grouping is further accentuated by their immersion into reggae, which asserts the positive aspects of an identity commonly devalued by society at large. The development of a separate and sometimes militant Black identity and the retention of Creole features in speech are thus the inevitable response to rejection, alienation and frustration.

Chapter 3

Verbal skills in West Indians

Reactions towards Creole can be paradoxical. When researchers with the Concept 7–9 project informally canvassed attitudes towards the language of West Indian children, it emerged that, on the one hand, teachers thought that they were non-verbal and inarticulate and that, on the other hand, they talked too much. In order to resolve such a paradox we need to understand the prejudices and stereotypes associated with both Creole and non-standard speech in general. It is only then that we can examine objectively the kind of verbal skills commonly found in West Indian children.

Standard and non-standard speech

Many people believe that all forms of non-standard speech are intrinsically inferior. They regularly describe them as 'sloppy', 'bad' and 'lazy' and hold that only standard English is 'proper' or 'correct'. Those who speak standard English with 'Received Pronunciation' are further considered to have 'a nice voice' or to be 'well spoken'.

Creole is generally felt to be a form of non-standard English, and consequently lacks prestige. Fagan (1958), for instance, in an analysis of the written work of Jamaican children gives a clear indication of popular prejudice when he describes Creole as 'merely broken English'. This is contrasted with 'good English', which 'has a beauty, charm and expressiveness that makes it capable of all that can be expected of a language in awakening the innermost thoughts and responses of the individual'. He also stresses the importance for Jamaican children to listen to 'high quality English' as often as possible since outside the school 'they rarely have such a privilege'.

The English language, however, does not have a monopoly of profound feeling or expressiveness. Fagan has made the mistake of equating the achievements of English literature with the intrinsic qualities of the language. It is important to remember that standard English is prestigious because it is associated with the socially powerful and that, from a linguistic viewpoint, it is a dialect like any other.

The development of standard English leaves us in little doubt about this. It is derived from dialects used in the south-east of England which gradually gained in status as London became the seat of government. Speakers at court, university scholars and, more recently, the public schools have all played a part over the centuries both in perpetuating its use and modifying its form. But the fact that the dialect of the upper classes of London developed into the most widely accepted form of the English language does not detract from its status as a dialect the same as any other. Had government been established in Newcastle, the Geordie dialect would now be considered standard English.

Non-standard English, on the other hand, has always been associated with the poorer members of society and has always lacked prestige. Attitudes towards it have tended to be so prejudiced that it is only in recent times that any serious attempt has been made to describe its many forms. Herskovits (1937), for instance, reports that until the late 1930s, the most common hypothesis proposed to account for Negro speech was that it was 'the blind groping of minds too primitive in modes of speech beyond their capabilities'.

With the arrival of printing it was inevitable that standard English should be in the form most widely used in books and that there should be little or no written material in non-standard dialects. Unfortunately, it is commonly held that the only 'real' languages with 'proper' grammars are those with a written literature. This overlooks the fact that the main purpose of writing is to provide a permanent record of speech and, in this sense, it must be regarded as a secondary development. It seems illogical, therefore, to consider a variety with little or no written literature to be any less valid as a language.

Verbal deprivation

Myths about non-standard English have been perpetuated for so long that many people find it very difficult to disentangle fact from fable. In educational circles over the past few decades the mythology has been given a veneer of academic respectability with the advent of theories of verbal deprivation. The claims of educationalists in this area have had considerable impact on both sides of the Atlantic and it is important, therefore, that they should be carefully examined.

Non-standard language is felt by many to be irregular, unsystematic and inadequate, and creoles are singled out for special scorn. Comments from some of the contributors to the report of the Birmingham branch of the Association of Teachers of English to Pupils from Overseas (ATEPO) (1970) on West Indian children clearly illustrate the common misconceptions. Their language is described as 'babyish', 'careless and slovenly', 'lacking proper grammar' and even 'very relaxed like the way they walk'. There is a 'glut of speech' but a 'poverty of correct expression' and they communicated 'by sign language'.

The fact remains, however, that statements of this kind are based on prejudice and not on observation and analysis. There is nothing to suggest that Creole or any other non-standard variety is irregular, faulty or unstructured. All languages can be shown in fact to consist of a highly structured set of patterns. It is not always possible to identify these patterns, but this is due to shortcomings in analysts and not in the language itself. The patterns are there to be discovered and often are of such complexity and precision that even the most sophisticated computer looks primitive in comparison.

We can illustrate this point by the Creole use of /ong/ for standard English /aʊn/ ('tong' for 'town'; 'brong' for 'brown'). On listening to a West Indian child the first impression is often that he vacillates between the Creole and the standard in a completely haphazard way. A closer examination, however, shows a very interesting pattern of restrictions. If, for instance, we take casual peer-group conversation, we find that the Creole use of /ong/ is proportionately far greater than the use of standard English /aʊn/; in a more formal situation, however, the situation is reversed. It is clear, therefore, that there are not two mutually exclusive systems at work, but that /ong/ is more likely to occur at the Creole end of the continuum and /aʊn/ at the standard end. It is not possible to predict categorically when a West Indian will choose one or the other, but this does not detract from the rule-governed nature of their behaviour. Patterns exist if we are sensitive enough to detect them.

Since this is the case it is difficult to understand how theories of verbal deprivation could ever have gained credibility. Part of the problem was that many of those who promoted the theories never actually observed the language of the 'verbally deprived' in a wide range of settings. Keller (1963), for instance, bases her ideas on answers to a questionnaire. And Bernstein, whose work we shall be considering in greater detail later, goes so far as to invent examples of his restricted and elaborated codes rather than quoting from actual speech. This approach is in direct contrast with that of linguists and anthropologists who have gained access to the homes of people in whom they are interested and have been able to observe them in a wide range of settings.

Labov, for instance, has always stressed the importance of situational restraints on speech. Both in Britain and in America there have been frequent reports that Black children give monosyllabic answers, or even grunts, in response to questions. Advocates of the verbal deprivation theory quote this as evidence for their case, but Labov (1972a) has demonstrated convincingly that this interpretation is extremely misleading. In transcripts of interviews with eight-year-old Leon, he shows first how little headway was made even though the interviewer was Black. Later, a more informal setting was created. Leon's best friend was invited to join in, they all sat on the floor eating crisps and sweets and the interviewer introduced taboo subjects into the conversation. The transformation was dramatic and it rapidly emerged that Leon was perfectly articulate.

Cognitive deficit

Many writers did not stop at the idea of verbal deprivation, but went on to postulate that children who were verbally deprived must also be cognitively deficient. The respect which linguists quite rightly have for the organizational powers of language not surprisingly makes them very suspicious of those who make such claims. Yet the notion of cognitive deficit has been widely accepted on both sides of the Atlantic, and owes a great deal to the work – or rather the misinterpretation of the work – of Bernstein.

Bernstein was the first to talk in terms of two polar codes – the 'elaborated code' and the 'restricted code' – which he postulated as two ideal types. In the light of evidence that working-class children are less likely to do well at all stages of education, he suggested that the different distribution of these two codes was a possible major cause. The elaborated code was claimed to exploit a much wider range of possibilities in both lexicon and syntax; its main function is to express relatively explicit meaning verbally. The restricted code, on the other hand, is seen as exploiting a narrower range of lexical and grammatical possibilities and making greater use of non-verbal channels. Bernstein suggests that different patterns of socialization are responsible for the development of these codes and that there are important cognitive implications. He considers, for instance, that the elaborated code gives access to 'universalistic' orders of meaning which are not context bound, whereas the restricted code gives access to 'particularistic' orders of meaning which are far more context bound. This leads him to believe that the restricted code restrains the processes of perception, thinking, remembering and learning.

Bernstein's early views appear to have been modified considerably over the years. At first it seemed that the division between working-class and middle-class speech corresponded to the division between the restricted and elaborated codes, although later articles correct this impression. More recently he has made a case for the teacher to be able to understand the child's dialect rather than trying to change it, and he stresses that he does not consider the working-class child to be linguistically deprived.

Unfortunately, many educationalists have understood Bernstein's theories of codes to apply equally to non-standard speech in such a way that the standard can be equated with the elaborated code and the non-standard with the restricted code. Bereiter *et al.* (1966), for instance, leave us in no doubt:

> Our estimation of the language of the culturally deprived children agrees with that of Bernstein, who maintains that this is not merely an undeveloped version of Standard English, but is a basically non-logical mode of expressive behaviour which lacks the formal properties for the organization of thought.

Yet linguistic analysis makes it quite clear that all languages and dialects provide for fundamental logical operations such as negation, conjunction, adjunction and deduction. The way in which these operations are carried out varies considerably from one language to the next, but there is no evidence that particular structures interfere with conceptualization. Nor is there evidence that some forms of language are better suited for abstract thought than others. It has never, in fact, been made clear what precisely constitutes the abstract thought of which non-standard speakers are allegedly incapable, though sometimes it is held to be the ability to generalize and categorize. But, by these criteria, all languages are equally suitable for expressing abstract thought, since speech is made possible only by internalized notions of grammatical category, and new utterances can only be formed by generalization from previously known patterns.

Confusion over Bernstein's intensions was partly responsible for the development of a large number of intervention programmes in America for children variously described as 'verbally deprived', 'culturally disadvantaged' or 'culturally deprived'. Not surprisingly, they never achieved the great successes that were heralded. The weaknesses which they set out to remedy have never been demonstrated; the children's language was clearly not standard English, but this does not mean that it was deficient.

Fortunately, no materials or educational programmes have been developed in Britain against this background of ignorance and prejudice. One project, however, Concept 7–9, can be mentioned conveniently at this point. Originally this was developed by the Schools Council as a language course for West Indian children, but its authors decided that many of the problems facing West Indians were shared by a large number of indigenous children and the emphasis was changed. They maintained that the language of West Indian and working-class White children was perfectly regular and logical, but they felt that non-standard speakers needed to develop a range of verbal strategies which would enable them to take part more successfully in the education process.

There seem to be two main problems in this approach. First, how are we to isolate the different verbal strategies necessary for educational success? The Bullock Report (1975, p. 67) identifies some eleven focuses for language development; Tough (1976) concentrates on seven main areas. The number of strategies that different authors arrive at seems quite arbitrary, and no convincing criteria have yet been suggested for deciding which are the most important. Second, can we be sure that children are not already competent users of these strategies in other situations? No reference is made in the report of the research phase of Concept 7–9 (Wight and Norris, 1970) to the child's use of language outside the classroom. Yet, as we have seen, the deficiencies which the American intervention programmes were trying to remedy were not to be found when the children were studied in a range of contexts.

Differences of style

Proponents of verbal deprivation and cognitive deficit seem to have overlooked the relationship between stylistic variation and social acceptability. Bernstein's elaborated and restricted codes appear to correspond to what linguists describe as differences of style, and different styles are suitable for different situations. Sometimes this is a question of formality. The language we use with family and friends is very different from the language of interviews or debating. At other times different styles can be related to the social background of the speakers. The public-school boy who for some reason decided to take a vacation job in a factory or on a building site would find himself socially ostracized if he did not make considerable adjustments in the direction of his workmates' speech. We may also associate a particular style with a particular subject so that, for instance, academic discussions are expected to take place in standard English.

But this does not mean that it would be impossible to use a non-standard variety. The fact that nearly all written material is in the standard somehow leads people to feel that non-standard English is incapable of conveying the same nuances, or entering the same degree of abstraction. Sutcliffe (1978) challenges these assumptions by writing a page of his thesis in Creole. In so doing he demonstrates that it is social acceptability and not linguistic inadequacy which excludes non-standard varieties from writing.

Disya a di laas paata wi raitin bout edyukieshan. Wi go luk aan di difran wie hou di langwij we wi taak mos impaatan fi di blak pikni-dem iina skuul.

Di likl paint-dem wi a mek nou — iina di mien piisa di buk a kom neks wi dis go tekop dem go taak bout dem fi mek taat fi eda piipl.

Dem aagyu bout langwij iina skuul langtaim, se a truu pikni taak mek dem laan, an se hou wen you main gruo-op, wen ya get muor kleva an ting, yu taakin fi gruo-op siem wie, di tuu dis tai-op tugyada. Aaftaword nou dem taat tingk bout di blak pikni Jamieka-taak an bout di wait pikni Hinglish-taak we dem faada wok iina faktri an ting

Bika demya pikni naa du gud iina skuul, rait?

Bot wi kyaan se a fi-dem langwij du dat-de. Wi kyaan se a hou di wod-dem komin an di piipl-dem yuusin dem fi stailin an dis an dat mek dem chupid. Bot eniwie disya aagyument gat tuu said, yu nuo. Bernstein-dem main gi dem se fi-wi langwij mashop, kyaan gud fi wi edyukieshan. Baratz an Labov an Stewart an Shuy se i no mashop i dis difran. A dis bika dem no taak laik fi-dem tiicha mekin plenti blak pikni kyaan gud iina skuul.

(In this final section of the survey we shall consider various aspects of language as they pertain to the education of West Indian children. The main body of the thesis which follows can be seen as a development of these brief points, or at least as a starting point from which to develop further.

47

Language has been a hotly debated issue in education for many years. Language is seen as central to education, and cognitive development is seen as inextricably linked with language development. Attention has then been turned to the language of working-class and ethnic-minority children, who as we have seen are tending to underachieve in school. A causal link has never been satisfactorily established between their language (its formal characteristics or its customary styles of use) and the poor performance. There are, none the less, two 'sides' to this debate: those, notably Bernstein, who hypothesize that there is something deficient in such language, at least as a preparation for academic education, and those such as Baratz, Labov, Stewart and Shuy, who maintain it is merely different — the difference between the language of the school causing all the educational difficulty. This debate is highly relevant to pupils from a Creole-speaking background.)

West Indians' view of their own speech

The discussion so far has centred on British attitudes towards West Indian and other non-standard varieties of speech. But negative attitudes towards non-standard speech are clearly not restricted to speakers of the standard variety, and non-standard speakers themselves are among the most severe critics. This pattern is one of the more unpleasant aspects of the domination of one group by another: the dominated are persuaded that they, their language and their culture are inferior and that the stigma attached to them is deserved.

Feelings of inferiority associated with Creole are apparent in all aspects of life. West Indians continually deprecate their speech. It is called 'broken', 'ugly', 'monkey talk', and Jamaicans are reminded that they will never amount to anything because they 'talk like Quashie'. These attitudes are a recurrent feature of West Indian literature, too. Lamming (1960), for instance, uses a character in *Season of Adventure* to express the sentiment:

She learn fast how to talk two ways ... Tonight she go talk great with the stranger man, grammar an' clause,

where do turn into does, plural an' singular in correct formation, an' all that. But inside her, like between you and
me, she tongue make the same rat-trap noise.

The outwardly negative reactions to Creole represent, however, only one facet of a very complex situation. Although, by
and large, West Indians seem to have accepted the critical
views expressed by standard speakers, Creole remains the
language of sincerity and is reserved for expressing strong
emotion. It is also something very personal and private and
can be used most effectively for excluding outsiders. This last
feeling was expressed very clearly by a West Indian girl in a
Midlands comprehensive school who had been asked the
meaning of some remark she had made in Creole. She waited
for the teacher to leave the room, then wrote on the black-
board: 'Sir is nosey about black people's language'. It is also
evident in the response of another West Indian child to a
teacher reading dialect poetry. Months later, in an essay
about likes and dislikes at school, 'Teachers talking West
Indian' was listed as one of his dislikes.

There is nothing remarkable about the ambivalent attitudes
of West Indians towards their language. Creole has been dep-
recated by people in authority since earliest times and its low
status has constantly been reinforced by the schools. It would
be far more remarkable if West Indians had emerged unscathed
after such an assault. But, on the other hand, Creole remains
a symbol of West Indian identity; it defines their membership
of a particular group with particular values and is the vehicle
of their culture. As such it is cherished and respected.

West Indian verbal skills

It is convenient to return now to our starting point: on the
one hand, teachers assert that West Indian children are inarticulate and non-verbal and, on the other hand, that they
talk too much. The range of verbal skills which operates in
the West Indies is in fact impressive and it may be of surprise
to the advocates of verbal deprivation that very great importance is attached to them. As in any pre-literate society, oral
traditions are highly prized, but the tendency of literate

societies to undervalue speech and assign status to the written word has often meant that rich verbal traditions have been overlooked by European observers. Verbal skills of West Indians in Britain tend to have been overlooked in the same way.

The great value attached to these verbal skills can be seen in the competitive element which is an integral element of many West Indian activities. Teasing and taunting tend to be very well developed even in quite young children. This, of course, is a universal activity, but in the West Indies it is highly stylized and can be regarded as something of an art form. It is certainly a talent widely found among West Indian children in British schools: take these interchanges between children at a Brixton primary school:

A: 'Hush you mouth.'
B: 'Why should I!'
A: 'Cos it's closing time.'
B: 'But I ain't a shop! So!'
A: 'I said shut you mouth.'
B: 'Why should I!'
A: 'Cos you lip long like frog.'
B: 'You don't talk about you own lip do you? You mouth favour the dog.'
A: 'A dog can eat off a frog! So!'
B: 'But a frog can jump over a dog! So! Take a mash and don't come flash! Take the shame and don't complain.'

In adolescents, especially adolescent males, these skills are developed still further and often find expression in 'rhyming' or what Black Americans call 'playing the dozens'. This is a battle of invective where one participant insults a member of the other's family – usually his mother – and the recipient returns the insult in kind. It is often a highly formalized exchange and sometimes rules are discussed before the battle begins. Most often the insults are in rhyme – hence the name 'rhyming'.

Ten crapaud (inedible frogs) was in a pan;
The bigger one was your mother man

Me and your mother in a pork barrel
And every word a give she a porky quarrel (i.e. made noise)

50

Me and your mother was digging potato
Spy under she and saw little Tobago

The entertainment value of the exchange is very important
and it is part of the mechanism whereby an individual gains
peer group status. They also provide an alternative to actual
fighting and Farb (1973) suggests that this was an important
development in a society where Blacks have been 'outnum-
bered and outgunned'.

In adults it is possible to make a distinction between the
'good talker' and the 'good arguer', who usually function in
completely different settings. The good talker is to be found
at the more serious community events – christenings, weddings, funerals, church and political meetings and thanks-
givings (given when a period of hardship has come to an end).
His means of expression are toasts, speeches or recitations.
There is also a wide range of well-established events which
allow the 'good arguer' to show off his talents. The many
carnivals and Mas'es, for instance, give rise to competing
troupes of players, although the form of these activities tends
to vary from island to island. In Tobago the 'Speech Band' is
composed of a hierarchy of individuals based on English
court, where rank depends on ability and experience at
speech making. Emphasis tends to be on team work rather
than virtuoso performance and all members have a chance to
take part. This contrasts with Trinidad where there is greater
stress on one outstanding performer.

The Nevis tea meetings provide an opportunity for the two
presiding chairmen to combine the talents of good talker and
good arguer. Abrahams (1970) describes these occasions as a
remarkable combination of pageant, mock fertility ritual,
variety show and organized mayhem, and the task of the
chairmen is indeed a formidable one. They take it in turns to
introduce each performer and compete to outshine the per-
formers with their interpolated remarks. The language is
ornate and highly rhetorical and is interspersed with more
and more Latin and latinate phrases as the meeting proceeds:

That song reminded me of Moses standing on the banks of
the Red Sea. It fills my heart with *phil-long-losophy,
entrong-losophy*, and *conomaltus*. Impro, imperium,
pompry, comilatus, allus comigotus, which is to say I come

51

here today without any study. Dia Gratia, by the grace of God, I have tried my best. Time is tempus fugit. The same. I will say a few words about Moses. His life he went into different parts; he spent forty years in Egypt, forty years in Medea, and forty years in the wilderness. I shall now sum bonum, malum cum shalltum propendum, peerum, desideratum, wobiteratum, attitaratin.

Orators, although attempting to 'confuse' (amaze) the audience by using big words which evoke favourable responses (laughter, applause, comments), are also careful not to 'confuse' them too much and so lose their attention. This requires considerable mental and verbal agility, as Charles Jack in Abrahams (1972) points out:

The moment decides and you have to be a quick thinker. And when you are in control, you must be able to know to think fast, what to do, how to do it, so that nobody vexed with you. And you get your call back [assent from the chairman or judges to proceed]. If they're vexed with you, you know, they'll start to heckle you. And when you start getting heckling, well you know the confusion. And when they confuse you, you know, that will make the end of the speaking.

In Nevis and St Kitts, there is a long tradition of archaic folk dramas which are of two main kinds: domestic farces and ritual combat plays. A feature of the combat plays is the battle of words which takes place between different champions, figures like David and Goliath, St George and the Turk and, more recently, Cowboys and Indians. Although most of these performances are prepared beforehand there is also opportunity for improvisation. Language tends to be highly metaphorical and ornate.

West Indians are often brilliant story-tellers and draw on skills which are usually unfamiliar to those of us who are used to reading or having stories read to us. Whereas written literature can assume a life of its own when it has left the author, oral narrative is heavily dependent on the interpretation of the story-teller and his interaction with the audience. He makes considerable use of stress, pauses, changes of rhythm, gestures and facial expression as he acts out the different episodes and roles. Members of the audience, for their part, may provide a running commentary, ask questions or even take over the lines of one of the characters. As in any pre-literate community, story-telling is a dramatic perform-ance and very much a community event.

Perhaps the best known of Caribbean folk tales are the Annancy stories, transported from West Africa largely un-changed. Annancy is a magic spider man who despite his size succeeds in getting the better of creatures much bigger and stronger, through his guile. It is not difficult to understand his appeal for an enslaved people and even today Annancy stories are part of the repertoire of all West Indians, adults and children alike. Louise Bennett, poet and actress, recalls how her grandmother used to tell her Annancy stories every night before she went to bed, repeating the songs in the story time and time again until she knew them and fell asleep sing-ing them to herself. At school children would swap Annancy stories during playtimes and lunch times and dramatic pres-entation was just as characteristic of children's performance as it was of adults' (Bennett, 1966, p. ix):

> It was sheer joy for us to recount how Annancy would 'talk wid tie-toung' (lisp) and say 'push' (put), 'yicky' (little) and 'sho' (so); and how Annancy would 'play fool fe ketch wise' (pretend to be stupid in order to outwit others) and 'study up him brains fe work brains pon people'.

Today Annancy thrives not only as the hero of folk tales but also in the theatre as the subject of song, verse and drama.

Dramatic presentation, however, is not restricted to folk tales. Sutcliffe (1978) in his study of West Indian children in Bedford notes a heightened narrative style with fast, fluent and rhythmic delivery, in a wide range of settings. To English ears this style — known as rapping or styling by Black Americans — sounds almost as though the speaker is singing. This is shown clearly in an extract from a conversation with Angela:

> And everybody a jumble round them. When they half way down London Road, you know down near that place down there, let me tell you one time they start a fight you

see, one piece of a fight! Me only stop to look they started to roll upon a ground you know. Roll! Let me tell you when they roll they really roll. Then they get up and start glaring at each other. About fifty people was round there an they was people standing outside them door a watch. So me walk home ... when me come to school on Monday morning, come from a place and there ah walk, when me find what the teacher come ask me for come stand up there with the headmaster there. Him send all of us, all of us down into him office and him take out him cane.

The West Indies also has a rich tradition of riddles. Although most English speaking communities tend to look upon them as a simple entertainment for children, many cultures regard riddles as a subtler education for life. This is a recurrent feature, for instance, of Greek mythology and other folk traditions; it is also to be seen in the Bible in stories like the Queen of Sheba's tests of Solomon's wisdom.

The West Indian riddle shows a marked African influence. Whereas most European riddles take the form of a question and answer sequence, the African riddle consists of some kind of cryptic description which refers to something else by analogy. The listener thinks about the description and then offers an explanation, although he has not explicitly been asked. The effect is often far more thoughtful and poetic than we are used to in the European tradition.

Sweet water standing up
A sugar cane

I have no life but I'm walking
A shadow

I went to town my face turned to town;
I came from town my face turned to town
Climbing a coconut tree

Proverbs, of course, are closely related to riddles: both are metaphorical, compress thought and express a general truth, though the proverb supplies both question and answer. Creole proverbs are plentiful. They are obviously concerned with the same general truths as any other culture, but they are often expressed in strikingly different ways.

Play with puppy, puppy lick your mouth
(Familiarity breeds contempt)

Near neighbour better than far brother
(A bird in hand is worth two in the bush)

Hot needle burn thread
(Haste makes waste)

It can be argued that many of the structural supports for West Indian verbal skills — tea meetings, carnival, mas'es — are absent from British society. None the less, many remain. Weddings, christenings and other community events allow the 'man of words' to show off his skills and West Indian church services are also important inasmuch as everyone is expected to be able to stand up and speak. Just as important, we are dealing with a dynamic, constantly changing situation and one fairly recent development in Jamaica, reggae, has had a considerable impact on the young Black population of Britain. Johnson (1976) considers the lyricism of reggae as 'part of, as well as being informed by, the wider Jamaican oral tradition', and for this reason it is included in the wider discussion of West Indian verbal skills.

Its themes are the everyday experience of large sections of the West Indian population — poverty, unemployment, homelessness, crime, rebellion. There is a marked religious symbolism, reminiscent of other West Indian verbal traditions, and songs are full of references to Babylon (police, oppressor, land of oppression); the Israelites (the repressed who are rebelling); Zion; Sodom and Gomorrah; Brimstone and Fire. But although the symbolism is usually religious, the sentiments expressed are most often political: it is not by accident that reggae has been called 'rebel music' and 'people's music'. This can be seen very clearly in the 'rudie' songs of the 1960s, a period characterized by considerable violence and political upheaval in Jamaica. Johnson describes a kind of lyrical dialectic whereby the 'Young Wailers' sang:

Jailhouse keeps empty
rudies get healthy
baton sticks get shorter
rudie gets taller
them fighting against the youth now
that's wrong
yout' a good, good rudie

and Mr Foundation, in 'All Rudies in Jail', replied:

Jailhouse them plenty
an' rudies getting scanty
baton sticks get taller
an' rudie getting shorter
they're fighting among themselves now
that's wrong
there's never been a good rudie

Originally, reggae strongly reflected its Jamaican origins, but more recently it has begun to deal with the situation of young Blacks in Britain and Troyna (1977a) points out that it is possible, for instance, to trace the deterioration of relations between police and young Blacks by following reggae records. Shortly after the Notting Hill confrontation during the 1976 carnival, a song about 'Police and youth in the Grove' appeared. Other lyrics and titles, including 'Streets of Ladbroke Grove', 'War in Babylon' and 'Fight to the End', reflect a growing political awareness of the situation of Blacks in Britain.

A parallel development concerns 'dub-lyricism'. This has been described as a 'new form of (oral) music poetry' (Johnson, 1976) in which rhythmic phrases are dubbed over the rhythm backgrounds of a popular song by the disc jockey. Themes are similar to those of reggae.

The discussion up to the present has been confined to oral skills. Of necessity, it has been brief and selective. It can hardly do justice to the range of skills which exists, nor can it adequately convey the great importance which West Indians attach to them. The emphasis on oracy, however, should not be taken to imply in any way that Creole has no place in literature. Any variety which has sustained a vital oral literature through numerous changes of culture (take, for example, the Annancy stories) is capable of sustaining a written literature, and there is a growing body of Creole literature. Louise Bennett in Jamaica and Linton Kwesi Johnson in London have produced a wide range of dialect poetry; V. S. Naipaul, Andrew Salkey and George Lamming have made skilful use of Creole dialogue in their novels; and some of the work of Samuel Selvon is written entirely in dialect. Observations on the inadequacy of the language of West Indian children in the light of evidence such as this are patently inappropriate: their language is certainly different, but by no means is it deficient.

Chapter 4

Creole Interference

Now that we have looked in detail at Creole and verbal skills in West Indians, we are in a better position to consider why precisely it might prove to be an obstacle to educational success. The discussion of the last two chapters has made it amply clear that there is nothing inherent in the structure of Creole which makes it inadequate or unsuitable as a vehicle of learning. It is possible, however, that Creole may 'interfere' with the production and comprehension of standard English.

'Interference' is a very common phenomenon in all kinds of learning activities. Psychologists talk about 'transfer' from one situation to another: sometimes this transfer is helpful or 'positive'; at other times it is unhelpful and 'interferes' with the task in hand. The problems encountered by motorists changing from one make of car to another provide a good illustration. The fact that they already know how to drive is a great advantage as there are certain basic principles no matter what the make of car. There are, however, differences between cars, which means that a certain amount of negative transfer, or interference, is inevitable. For instance, when the driver changes cars he may press a lever on the right expecting his indicator to start working, and be surprised when he sees the windscreen wipers going back and forth; or he may apply the same amount of pressure to the brakes as he usually does, only to find himself grinding to a sudden halt.

Similarly, in language, we are all familiar with the French speaker who says 'zees' for 'this', or with our own difficulty in pronouncing the French 'u' in 'tu'. Nor is linguistic interference restricted to sound systems; it can occur in grammar and vocabulary, too. We tend to think that because Creole is based largely on English vocabulary and shares many features with English that interference will not constitute a major problem. But the mere fact that the two varieties are closely related can pose difficulties. In Chapter 2 we pointed out the many structural differences between Creole and British English, but we also drew attention to suffixes, words and constructions common to the two varieties but used quite differently. Although a situation like this seldom results in total non-comprehension, it may quite often lead to partial understanding. And the fact that neither party suspects a communication problem makes this more likely still.

It is proposed in this chapter to look at the different ways in which interference of this kind may lead to educational problems. This is not to suggest, however, that all, or even most, West Indians are seriously handicapped by their Creole background. The extent of Creole interference will be seen to vary enormously from individual to individual, but none the less it is important to look closely at the special difficulties which face many Creole speakers. Nor is it proposed to look at language in isolation. The possibility that teachers' attitudes to linguistic differences may play a bigger part in the children's underperformance than the differences themselves will be given serious consideration.

Interference in speech

This is an extremely important area. It was suggested in Chapter 2 that relatively few children are truly bidialectal in so much as they have total control of two different systems. The situation is rather that there is constant interference between one part of the Creole-standard continuum and another. The way in which the teacher reacts to this interference in speech is of such vital importance that it is dealt with separately elsewhere in this book. (Chapter 5 will look at the actual mechanism of linguistic stereotyping and its implications for educational success; Chapter 6 will consider different pedagogic approaches to the situation.) It will be suggested that a child's speech is something intensely personal and that any criticism of the way he talks will be perceived as a criticism of the child himself. By the same token it will be suggested that any attempt to change the child's speech patterns will be harmful and counterproductive.

Interference in understanding speech

The speech of a child who has recently arrived from the Caribbean or who has just started in the reception class may be incomprehensible even to a teacher who has had a good deal of contact with West Indian children. For some reason it does not always occur to the teacher that the child may be experiencing difficulties just as great in understanding her. These difficulties can be particularly distressing if children are not expecting any kind of language barrier. Many West Indians refuse to admit that they speak anything other than 'English'. This results partly from the fact that they have been indoctrinated into believing that Creole is an inferior, 'broken' form of English; and partly from a very strong feeling of the Englishness of their heritage. Questions about language thus often provoke defensive reactions on the part of West Indians. And it is very unlikely that their children are prepared for the kind of difficulties which they are likely to face in the same way as, for instance, Indian or Cypriot children.

The sources of difficulty are numerous: different grammar, different vocabulary and, especially on first arrival, different sound systems. We all learn to distinguish only those sounds which are meaningful in our own language or dialect. Thus Spanish and French speakers have great difficulty in distinguishing between English 'kin' and 'keen'. Similarly, English speakers find it impossible to distinguish between the Gujerati words (t^haru) and (taru). These words differ only in the aspiration of the first letter but because this distinction is not important in English, English speakers consistently fail to tell the words apart. Yet for Gujeratis this is important enough to mark the difference between *your* and *thought*. The problem is one of perception – we perceive only those sounds which are meaningful in our own sound system.

A period of considerable adjustment for both teacher and child is bound to arise. And even when the child perceives the words correctly they may have different meanings, and certain constructions may prove puzzling. Nor do difficulties have to be very numerous to cause confusion. One key word or expression can completely 'throw' the listener. One West Indian describes vividly her frustrations during a schools broadcast on moths shortly after her arrival from St Kitts (*Observer* Magazine, 16 December 1973):

> 'The teacher thought I was thick, but I didn't know what a moth was. If she had said butterfly or something it would have been different.' Consequently, she only understood a word here and there in that lesson — 'the sound was pouring over my ears but I couldn't catch the sense of it'.

In one respect, then, the Creole-speaking child may be at an even greater disadvantage than, for instance, the Punjabi- or Chinese-speaking child in the British school. Both child and teacher accept that they are speaking different languages, are prepared for difficulties and adjust their communication techniques accordingly. But in the case of the Creole-speaking child there are many situations in which there may be complete misunderstanding or, more likely, partial understanding. The common assumption that West Indians speak 'English' may lead both speaker and addressee to think that the message has been communicated successfully when this is not in fact the case.

Such are the problems of children new to the situation. A typical teacher response is to rephrase a request or a question several times in the hope that the child will eventually understand. But verbal bombardment is far less likely to help than showing the child what is required or using another West Indian child to explain. The unconscious tendency to raise your voice when faced with a person who does not understand is likely to be less helpful still. But the greater danger in this situation is that the teacher should decide that the child is stupid or slow when he gives the wrong response or no response at all. This may be communicated to the child by dismissive words and gestures or simply by a lack of interest. The result is potentially disastrous, as the review of research on teacher expectations in Chapter 5 will show.

It has already been suggested that the situation is most acute in reception classes and when children have arrived recently from the Caribbean. But this does not mean that difficulties disappear within a few months of contact with the British school system. Young (1973) expresses the dilemma of many West Indian children very clearly, suggesting that they may often experience a kind of 'comprehension lag':

> The child unfamiliar with [the standard] has to catch up on what has been said, while the teacher is already going on to another point. In such a situation, the child may simply stop making the effort to catch up and so fall further behind, both in actual educational progress and ability to understand what is taught. To make matters worse, the teacher may then decide that such a child is simply dull, perhaps 'unteachable' rather than suffering through no fault of his own from a communication problem.

Interference in writing

The written work of West Indian children shows ample evidence of Creole interference. Unfortunately, especially in the early years of schooling, more general problems of literacy tend to mask the special problems of dialect interference and, unless the teacher is sensitive to the differences between Creole and British English, 'mistakes' attributable to the child's own linguistic system are likely to be interpreted as a far more serious literacy problem than actually exists.

Interference is to be seen both in the transfer of Creole grammar to the children's written work and in the spellings which reflect Creole phonology. Dealing first with the question of spelling, we find many of the features of the Creole sound system in the writing of West Indian children, though the extent of this kind of interference varies enormously from child to child, and is certainly more marked in younger children. A survey of the written work of children in two primary schools and a comprehensive school in Reading revealed frequent spellings of the kind listed below:

Creole /t, d/; English /th/

He was very *tin* and he was very dirty (Alison, 9)
There is about *tree* (three) kinds of zebra are left in Africa
(Donna, 10)

Creole /θ/; English /ð/

One day Michael set out *fram* (from) home to look *far*
(for) advencher (Gary, 8)
Shrimps are about 6 cm *lang* (long) (Kevin, 9)

Creole /a/; English /ɔ/

'How *dear* (dare) she', said Hilda (Jennifer, 13)
I went *downstiars* (downstairs) (Paula, 7)

This last example, of course, may well be a simple reversal,
but the fact that this was not a regular feature of Paula's
work suggests that *downstiars* should be explained in terms
of Creole interference.

Reduction of consonant clusters at the end of words

I will *fine* (find) them (Alison, 9)
He forgot wher she lived and had to go *pars* (past) a vicar
(Kevin, 9)

This kind of phonological interference seems to be a lot less
evident in the work of older children, though it certainly has
not disappeared altogether. It was very noticeable in the
primary school which used the initial teaching alphabet (i.t.a.)
and we shall be considering the implications of this later, in
Chapter 6. The problems which face West Indian children in
spelling English are not, of course, unique. English orthography does not match any pronunciation system very closely
and every learner has to match his own pronunciation system
to the spelling. Children in south-east England, for instance,
make frequent mistakes in spelling words like *there* and *their*

because they are pronounced the same. Children from South Wales, on the other hand, have no difficulty because they pronounce them differently (/δε/ and /δεyə/). If we delve a little further, however, we find that pairs of words like *year* and *ear*, and *coat* and *court*, are pronounced alike by the Welsh children, and it emerges that no one dialect has a monopoly of advantages or disadvantages over any other.

Although it might be argued that the West Indian child has to adapt to a slightly greater extent than speakers of other regional dialects of English, there is no reason why this should pose an insuperable barrier to literacy. The teacher's familiarity with the West Indian child's sound system and his reaction to dialect-based misspellings are, however, crucial. If the teacher does not recognize the source of the child's difficulties he is likely to imagine that his literacy problems are far greater than they are in fact, and to be ready to label him as 'dyslexic', 'slow' or 'hopeless'. Similarly, if the teacher is constantly 'correcting' the child in a state of ignorance of the regularities in spelling mistakes, the result is likely to be a lack of confidence and confusion on the part of the child. There is a great deal of evidence in the written work of West Indian children that this is often the case. Many children seem to have a vague notion as to what they are doing wrong: they know that they frequently write *t* where the teacher wants *th*; they realize that they frequently leave off the endings of words. But in the absence of clear and systematic explanations of the differences between Creole and standard English they tend to overgeneralize and hypercorrect. And, whereas Creole influenced spellings are more particularly a feature of the writings of younger children, hypercorrections seem to be found in greater numbers as the children get older. Below are some examples of the kind of hypercorrection which occurs:

> Mens down in the quarry found *stonds* (stones) (Kevin, 9)
> *Guest* (guess) what (Alison, 13)
> I could not find my *past* (pass) (Andrea, 14)
> I was going down the road one day and *thereupond* (thereupon) I met a bear (Donna, 10)
> He got the tools from the *booth* (boot) and put his keys back in his coat pocket (Erma, 14)

Grammatical interference

Grammatical interference in the written work of West Indian children is very common, though it should be mentioned that some of the features we will be discussing also appear in the work of English children. Occasionally an English child will write *six dog* or *he jump over the fence* and the most likely explanation is that this is a careless mistake. The same may be true of a West Indian child but several considerations suggest this is not often the case. First, West Indian children make this kind of 'mistake' far more frequently than their English peers. Second, 'mistakes' persist throughout the age range, whereas they are concentrated mainly in the work of younger English children. Finally, they can be explained in terms of West Indian speech patterns, so that there is evidence that these are perfectly regular linguistic structures rather than careless mistakes.

Some examples of grammatical interference are more readily recognized than others. These include plurals, the use of past tenses and subject-verb agreement – the features which were singled out in fact in the Concept 7–9 Dialect Kit for special attention because they remained the most persistent features in the children's written work. Examples such as those below are familiar to any teacher who has worked with West Indian children, few of whom would fail to recognize the child's native dialect as the source of interference.

One day their live a witct and her husband and five little *girl* (Karen, 8)
Don't stand they Alfred and let this woman call me *name* (Jennifer, 13)
One Christmas day father Christmas he *give* me a present for Christmas (Sharon, 6)
He had six wifes and he *chop* of the head of the sixth one (Gillian, 8)
Minerva *know* all about spiders (Lloyd, 8)
Mary usually *sleep* on my bed (Valerie, 14)

It comes as something of a surprise that features such as these are still to be found in the written work of secondary age children. They are among the most stigmatized features of West Indian speech; they have been 'corrected' by generations of teachers in the West Indies and continue to meet with censure in British schools. Given this, and the amount of exposure to the British model in both writing and speech, it seems amazing that these features are so remarkably persistent.

There are two possible contributory factors. First, contrary to common assumption, all West Indians do use the *-s* suffix of the plural and the *-ed* suffix of the past tense on some occasions. If you examine West Indian speech, it emerges that standard forms are found more frequently, though by no means exclusively, in formal situations than in casual conversation with family and friends; and that these suffixes are to be found in the speech of all West Indians on some occasions. Whereas the English child has an almost invariable rule whereby, for instance, *-s* is added to plural nouns or *-ed* to the past tense form of weak verbs, a much more complex system is in operation for the West Indian child. The standard form is triggered by formality and context, and even then the relationship is not of a one-to-one kind. It is not a question of adding the suffix to indicate formality, but of using it proportionately more often to show that the situation is more formal. If you compare samples of the speech of West Indians with samples of their written work, for instance, you are likely to find a greater incidence of standard forms in their written work. In this sense, they have already recognized the greater formality of writing, a rule system is in fact in operation and the alternation between standard and non-standard forms is not nearly as haphazard as it might seem.

A second possible explanation of why Creole forms persist in the language of West Indian children is a semi-conscious decision to preserve their separate identity. Many teachers have noticed how a child with very few Creole features in his speech at primary school has acquired a marked West Indian accent by the time he reaches adolescence. Although it is doubtful if linguistic patterns are adopted on a conscious level, the social implications are far-reaching. Adoption of standard forms acknowledges acceptance of the values of those who use the standard language; retention of Creole features indicates membership of a particular cultural and linguistic group and rejection of the values associated with standard speakers.

66

Features such as plurals and past tenses are often approached with very *ad hoc* teaching methods. Teachers unaware of the patterns of Creole or their significance — social or linguistic — can be very inconsistent in the way in which they tackle the problem. On numerous occasions during a survey of marking strategies in the work of West Indian children, there seemed to be an entirely arbitrary approach. In this piece of work by a ten-year-old West Indian

It look's very good
It smell creamy
It's very smooth texture
It's very brown
It stand like a stone
It smell like milk

the only alteration was to the second line where the teacher changed *smell* to *smells*. It is difficult to imagine, however, what conclusions the West Indian child is supposed to draw when the teacher has chosen to add *-s* to *smell* but not to *stand*, nor indeed to *smell* when it reappears in the last line. The same observation can be made of many teachers' handling of the *-ed* suffix of the past tense and other Creole features.

As in the case of Creole interference in spelling, a frequent consequence of *ad hoc* teaching strategies is overgeneralization and hypercorrection. This is to be seen to some extent in normal Creole situations where the hypercorrected form has become the norm (cf. *teeth, peas, shoes* ... which do not exist in the singular). But in a British context this phenomenon is far more widespread and much more idiosyncratic.

They saw a *seaplanes* land in the sea (Colin, 9)
All of them were cheering for the *mices* (Gillian, 8)
We *standed* by a painted picture (Kevin, 9)
They *fighted* and Robin wone (Donna, 10)
It *haves* big long wings (Peter, 9)
The slides *makes* the sugar canes *turns* into the box (Paul, 6)

It would appear, then, that the teacher should exercise very great caution in the 'correction' of such features. It is not simply a matter of reminding a child when you have the time that *dogs* has an 's' on it when we are talking about more than one dog. The differences need to be explained

67

systematically and consistently and, as we shall discuss later, it is possible to argue that such explanations should be postponed until the child's literacy is firmly founded on his own speech patterns. But, even more important, a failure to adopt a standard form should never be interpreted as a sign of 'dullness' in a child. What to us is simply an either-or situation is far more complex for a West Indian child: his choice may be affected by contextual considerations, or even identity.

So far we have discussed only those features considered to be the most persistent in the speech and writing of West Indian children by the Concept 7–9 research team. A number of other features, however, also occur quite regularly in the language of West Indian children, and one such feature is the Creole treatment of possessives:

> *Craig father* took *Caledonia stick* and trieded to get the parokeets (Karen, 8)
> He never took one of the *man sheep* (Donovan, 10)
> So he went to his *friend house* and asked him if he would like to try out his new car (Erma, 14)

Hypercorrection is seen here, too, in examples like

> *Jane's dad's* was a detective (Peter, 9)

Another common feature, the use of multiple negation, is shared, of course, with many working-class English children:

> It was *not nowhere* to be seen (Colin, 9)
> He did *not* see *no-one* to sker (Donna, 10)
> *No-one* was *not* at home (Donovan, 10)

Other features, however, are exclusively West Indian. It has already been mentioned, for instance, that Creole uses the standard English active form of the verb to express both active and passive standard meanings:

> *It pick* when it 5 years old (Kevin, 9)
> Some food you have to chew and some just *swallow* straight away (Angela, 12)
> Some had to stay to have their picker *take* (Donna, 10)

But almost as frequent as examples of actual Creole usage are blends of the standard and Creole, and overgeneralized forms:

They say nothing was broke but it would need *bandej up*
(Donna, 10)
It got *eated* up by a wild dog (Peter, 9)
It is *sticked* with its sticky legs (Allison, 9)

Another feature of Creole is the zero copula: it is possible
for the subject of a sentence to be followed directly by a verb,
an adjective and, occasionally, a noun or a locative, without
using the verb *to be*. The following are examples of some of
the possibilities:

Everyone *swimming* in the pool (Roslyn, 10)
I *going* swimming to the Limpopo river (Lloyd, 6)
It *frightening* and it scarey (Paul, 6)
He came to the man house when he *asleep* (Michael, 10)
It *dinosaurs* dad said tim (Donovan, 10)
Eight o'clock *my bed time* (Alison, 9)

It is seldom commented upon that many words common to
British English and Creole are used as different parts of speech
in the two varieties:

Paul *handstand* with me (Alison, 9)
I would *suicide* myself (Donna, 10)
It was a Saturday when my dad was going to *sale* his car
(Erma, 14)

This tendency is particularly marked in the Creole use of
adverbs:

We all live *happy* ever after (Pauline, 10)
I was watching John Curry how *good* he ice-skate (Donna,
10)

Donna's last example also illustrates another Creole feature.
Clause construction is sometimes quite different in Creole
and this often results in sentences which sound distinctly un-
English:

Long time, *the man* in London *he* had to go away for a
very long time (Kevin, 9)
They did not know what to do, *if to go in or to stay out*
(Jennifer, 14)

Particular problems with verbs

We have already discussed some aspects of Creole interference in verbs. Examples have been given which show how the un-marked Creole form appears in a variety of situations – third person singular present, past tenses, passives – and this is a feature which has been commented on at some considerable length in descriptions of language in the West Indies. It has also been suggested that this is an area which gives rise to a good deal of hypercorrection in children's written work. But no reference has been made to an area of great difficulty for many West Indian children – the English sequence of tenses.

> The mountain lion *did not see* where he *can go* (Michael, 10)
> I *was* five minutes late already so I hoped the bus *will come* soon (Andrea, 14)
> We *will go* in to see what it *would be* like (Donna, 10)

Examples such as these are to be found frequently in the work of large numbers of West Indian children. The particular nature of their difficulty, however, is to be seen more clearly in a more extended piece of writing (Pauline, 10):

> When I go to bed at night I turned off the light. I put my head on the sheet. That time I was very scared all by my-self in the middle of the night and you couldn't see any-thing. Some time when I turned off the light I saw the twinkling star through the window and then I started to look at it nearly all the time, then suddenly my eyes start to burn me that means I wanted to sleep and then I clouse my eyes and went to sleep.

The teacher's comment, 'Tenses mixed up', is not likely to be of much help to the child concerned. She shows a remarkable inconsistency and vacillates between present and past tenses, although only the present is required. Her writing points to linguistic insecurity and confusion. It is not difficult to imagine a situation in which her unmarked Creole forms have been repeatedly 'corrected' by her teachers without any clear or consistent explanation of why this should be the case. She has reached a point where she uses past tenses even when they are not necessary, at least some of the time.

Another difficulty involving verbs is the number of forms which appear in West Indian children's work which can be attributed neither to English nor to Creole and which cannot easily be explained in terms of hypercorrection:

Try to don't broke my vase said the lady (Jennifer, 14)
John was lead the dinosaur (Glenroy, 10)
I am always helps my mother (Derry, 8)
I *was happen* to be looking through the curtains (Jennifer, 14)
The Scotland people *keep on say* that they *does be see* a monster in a river could Lochness (Colin, 9)

The work of these children is a very powerful argument against correcting 'mistakes'. In the early stages of literacy the child is particularly vulnerable and, as I shall be arguing later, it is far more realistic to postpone comparisons with standard English to a later stage. The young child is not equipped to understand teachers' references to 'past tenses' and 'third person singulars'; the teacher seldom has the vocabulary or the linguistic knowledge to describe them in terms which might be more meaningful to the child. This often results in inconsistent and incoherent marking procedures on the part of the teacher, and confusion and uncertainty on the part of the child.

Incidence of broad Creole forms

One final area needs to be discussed: the incidence of broad Creole forms. It is commonly assumed that the most extreme elements of Creole are rapidly eliminated from the written work of West Indian children. Yet some of the features normally associated with the lower end of the Creole-English continuum are to be found even in the work of children born in this country. This is not to suggest that these extreme forms occur frequently or that all or most West Indian children use them. None the less, the small sample considered for the purpose of the present analysis revealed a wide range of features that are normally considered broad Creole, including the examples listed below.

71

Creole plural marker 'de ... dem'

The people *them* was their and they jump in the house and
they start fight (Donovan, 10)
And *the* man *them* said by the time they must reach the
house it will burn down (Donovan, 10)

Pronouns

While they were going to get him *them* told other people
what they had seen (Colin, 9)
This time they making *they* house with brick (Cora, 10)
The baby cry until *it* mother Estha brote it upstaire and
pot it to sleep (Paula, 6)

Vocabulary

After that they burn it and then they *mashed* (destroyed)
it (Paul, 6)
Tim run to his mother can I keep John O mum I no a lat
about dinosaur well I said no *I and I* mean no so go home
(Cora, 10)
The baby *name* Robert (Andrea, 14)
Is a island *name* B.P. bay (There is an island called B.P.
bay) (Kevin, 9)

Concatenation of verbs

In 1966 the gang *came and go* into the shop and take out
something and don't pay for it (Donovan, 10)

Several conclusions can be drawn from this brief analysis
of children's written work. First, there is extensive evidence
of interference from Creole. Out of a sample of thirty children's work only three showed no evidence at all of Creole
influence and, although the rest of the sample varied considerably in the degree of interference, at least a quarter of
the children showed extensive interference on all levels. It is
also interesting that these children came from schools in

Reading where the proportion of West Indian children varied between 20 and 40 per cent. It seems feasible to assume that in schools where the proportion of West Indian children is higher, the number of children whose work is heavily influenced by Creole will be higher still. Second, the extent of hypercorrect and overgeneralized forms in the children's work points to a considerable degree of confusion and linguistic insecurity. Inconsistency and a failure systematically to explain differences between Creole and British English on the part of the teacher must surely have played a large part in producing this state. Finally, there seems little evidence to support the position taken by some writers that bidialectalism has largely been achieved.

Reading

The various trends in the teaching of reading over the last few decades reflect a very great uncertainty as to what is involved in the reading process. One of the most controversial issues in this area is the importance which should be attached to reading with understanding. Thus, phonic and alphabetic approaches are concerned with the association of letters and sounds (or letter names) to the exclusion of meaning; in this view, reading is a precise sequential process. Word methods like 'Look and Say' and language experience approaches like 'Breakthrough to Literacy', on the other hand, emphasize comprehension and pay less attention to letter-sound relationships.

Although in practice every method draws to some extent on the insights of others, and there is general acceptance that no single approach holds the key to the process of learning to read, the emphasis has shifted very firmly in recent years to the need for reading with understanding. This has come about as a result of an increasing body of information which demonstrates that fluent reading is not simply a matter of decoding sequential relationships.

Studies of competent readers show that words are not perceived in a strictly linear sequence. Using highly complex photographic equipment, it is possible to follow the eyes as they move about the text, scanning backwards and forwards.

This suggests that the reader identifies only key words and phrases and that the brain rapidly infers any missing information before constructing the whole into a meaningful message. This is certainly consistent with the facts of silent reading. The same passage can take up to four times as long when read aloud, which indicates that the silent reader does not have time to process every word, let alone every letter.

Research undertaken on oral reading errors or miscues confirms the hypothesis that reading is not a precise sequential process. Goodman (1972) sees it rather as a 'psycholinguistic guessing game' which he explains in these terms:

> Reading is a selective process. It involves partial use of minimal language cues selected from perceptual input on the basis of the reader's expectation. As this partial information is processed, tentative decisions are made to be confirmed, rejected and refined as reading progresses.

He points out that if a child substitutes 'the' for 'your' it is obviously not because of the graphic similarity between the two words. They do, however, share a grammatical function inasmuch as they can both stand before nouns (*the book; your book*). What is more, the substitution of 'the' for 'your' need not affect the grammar or the meaning of the passage.

Miscue analysis of this kind has enabled Goodman to arrive at a model of the reading process which he believes to be powerful enough to predict and explain reading behaviour. The brain is seen as an information processing centre. It initiates the activity, it predicts and seeks order in the material, confirming predictions and correcting inconsistencies. Then it terminates the process when the task is completed, non-productive or boring, and so on. Reading with understanding is essential to this interpretation, and any attempt which does not end with meaning is classed as a 'short circuit'.

Smith (1971; 1973), Kolers (1973) and several other writers put forward a similar case and supply additional evidence. All these researchers envisage the reading process as heavily dependent on cue systems of various kinds. Some rely on the reader's grammatical knowledge. Thus, within the word there are many different suffixes which help identify the part of speech or form class. These include tense markers like *-ed*, plural markers like *-s*, noun markers like *-tion* and adjective markers like *-ish*. In sentences and discourse word order gives important clues so that in the example

John and Peter X the dog

X can only be interpreted as a verb. The reader will also make use of graphical information – letter-sound relationships, known word parts, recurrent spelling patterns, redundancies. And, finally, he will draw on a whole range of extra-linguistic cues, including pictures, concrete objects, the teacher's prompting and his prior experience of life and learning. Cues such as these, then, provide the input which allows the reader to select and predict, and are seen as essential for reading with meaning.

If we accept this model there are many potential difficulties for the West Indian child influenced by Creole who is faced with a reading passage in standard English. His cue system is quite clearly very different from that of an English child. As we saw in Chapter 2, some words and constructions are peculiar to Creole; others are common to Creole and English but are used in distinct ways. And certain suffixes mark one form class in Creole and another in British English. Cues relating to word order might also be interpreted differently. Thus, the English child who sees a noun at the beginning of a sentence or a clause knows that in all probability the next word will be a verb. The West Indian influenced by Creole, however, would have no reason to prefer a verb to an adjective, locative or noun, since all are possible in his linguistic code. Again, the experience which he brings with him to the classroom is often very different from that of his English peers. All these possibilities make the task of reading with understanding potentially difficult.

There is some disagreement as to how large a part dialect plays in hindering the reading process. Originally, Goodman (1965) suggested that there would be a direct relationship between the degree of dialect divergence and success in learning to read. In the light of subsequent research, however, he feels that the most realistic explanation of reading failure in non-standard speakers is rejection of their dialect by the schools. He points out that dialect involved miscues in oral reading do not interfere with the reading process or the construction of meaning, since they demonstrate that readers have grasped the meaning sufficiently to have been able to translate the standard form into their own dialect. Thus if a child reads

Freddie father walk home last night

for

Freddie's father walked home last night

he has shown convincingly that he has understood the sentence. Goodman and Buck (1973) suggest instead that the only special disadvantage which dialect speakers suffer in learning to read is one imposed by the school. Any dialect-based miscue which the teacher 'corrects' moves the reader away from using his linguistic competence in getting at the meaning of the text. The main aim becomes word-for-word accuracy rather than meaning.

It would seem that Goodman's position is a realistic statement of the situation of West Indian children learning to read in Britain. Jim Wight, who directed the Schools Council Project on teaching English to West Indian children, began work on a new project ('Reading with understanding') with the hypothesis that at the infant stage differences between the West Indian child's language and that of his reading books might seriously influence the speed at which literacy can be achieved. Although the research undertaken for this project was by no means exhaustive, no evidence of dialect-related difficulties was uncovered. Wight, like Goodman, sees the main problem as the school's attitudes towards the children's language rather than the actual language differences.

Both Goodman and Wight have been concerned with early readers. There are indications, however, that beginning and advanced reading are very different activities and it seems possible that dialect may only begin to pose serious difficulties in the later stages of reading. Shuy (1975) holds that more behavioural processes, like letter-sound associations, are dominant in early readers and that as they become more and more proficient they call increasingly on cognitive strategies which involve processing larger and larger stretches of language. He suggests that once the child progresses beyond the more mechanical aspects of reading and begins to process at sentence and discourse level the similarities between the language used in real life and the language of the text he is reading become less and less well defined. Mismatches between spoken and written language may hamper the proper processing of clues, especially in the reader who has mastered the mechanical skills of reading sufficiently to call on them less and less.

Research undertaken by the present writer, Edwards (1975), certainly supports this interpretation. Forty West Indian and forty English children in their first year of secondary school were matched for reading performance using the Neale Analysis of Reading Ability and their answers to comprehension questions based on the texts they had read were compared. Several important findings emerged. First, significant differences were found between West Indian and English subjects, but only in the case of good and average readers.

Mean comprehension ages

	English children	West Indian children	Significance
Poor readers	8 yrs 4 mths	8 yrs 4 mths	not sig.
Average readers	11 yrs 6 mths	9 yrs 8 mths	1%
Good readers	12 yrs 3 mths	10 yrs 6 mths	5%

Although there is no difference between the mean comprehension ages of the two groups of poor readers, the difference between the mean scores of English and West Indian average readers is striking. Very few of the West Indian subjects performed at the same level as the British children. The scores of the West Indian good readers, however, reflect a rather different pattern. Those children who underperform tend to score very low indeed, but there is a much larger number who perform completely satisfactorily and the indications are that they are perfectly bidialectal.

It is interesting that no differences were found between the two groups of poor readers. These were children who only completed passages one and two and, in some cases, passage three, of six progressively difficult passages, and this would seem to confirm the position of Wight and Goodman that dialect does not interfere with the initial stages of reading.

	Passage 1	Passage 2	Passage 3	Passage 4	Passage 5	Passage 6
Poor readers						
West Indian mean	3.62	7.18	3.75			
English mean	3.62	6.92	4.57			
Significance	n.s.	n.s.	n.s.			
Average readers						
West Indian mean	3.55	6.45	3.45	3.27	1.88	2.80
English mean	3.67	7.67	6.00	6.08	6.63	5.57
Significance	n.s.	n.s.	1%	h.s.	5%	1%
Good readers						
West Indian mean	3.63	6.31	4.50	4.31	3.13	3.06
English mean	3.93	7.13	6.47	6.27	6.27	6.40
Significance	n.s.	n.s.	h.s.	5%	1%	1%

n.s. = not significant
h.s. = highly significant

This can be seen even more clearly in a passage-by-passage analysis of comprehension scores. It can be seen that the differences between the two groups become more marked as the passages call for more cognitive styles of processing, and as they become more linguistically remote from Creole. Thus no differences emerged on the first two texts but a pattern of increasing significance was to be seen in successive passages. A similar study undertaken by Smolins (1974) adds weight to this argument. Here the children were much younger and their reading performance was concentrated in the first three passages. The difference between West Indian and English scores was considerably smaller than in the Edwards study.

But although dialect does not seem to interfere with the acquisition of reading skills, the data reported above, and evidence from other studies, suggest that it may become an important factor in the later stages of reading. The places at which readers hesitate give us an important clue. Fluent readers pause only at grammatical junctures (marked graphically by full stops, commas, semi-colons, etc.). But an analysis of the oral reading reported above showed some interesting trends. Although there was no significant difference between the two groups of poor readers, good and average West Indian readers were found to pause considerably more often at non-grammatical junctures than their British counterparts.

The Neale Analysis counts as errors only words which are misread or unattempted. The West Indian children, therefore, appeared to be performing on a par with their English counterparts. Yet they paused more frequently at non-grammatical junctures, which suggests that they are not as skilful at the sampling and hypothesizing techniques which we have been discussing. Since one's ability to hypothesize depends on one's familiarity with the structure of the language, it would seem that the greater frequency of hesitation in West Indian subjects is due in part at least to interference from Creole and it may be this which is ultimately responsible for the fact that they perform worse on comprehension tasks as a whole than the English subjects.

Results from supplementary tests devised to assess the degree to which West Indian children are influenced by Creole showed that there was a very definite relationship between performance on comprehension tasks and dialect interference. The tests were in the form of a multiple-choice questionnaire: in response to a cue sentence subjects were asked to select one of three possibilities, of which at least one was appropriate in a British context, and at least one in a Creole context.

I was looking for my book but when I went into the bedroom all I could see was Jane's.
What could I see?
(a) Jane
(b) Two girls called Jane
(c) Jane's book
(Test for understanding of possessives)
Impalas eat often at this time of the year.
(a) Yes, they taste nice
(b) Yes, they eat a lot of food
(c) Yes, they give a lot to eat
(Test for understanding of passives)

It emerged that those children who were influenced a great deal by Creole had low scores on the comprehension tasks, which strongly suggests that differences between Creole and English can cause considerable difficulty for some West Indians in the later stages of reading.

Another finding which emerged from this research was that West Indian children born in this country and those who have arrived from the Caribbean more recently could only be separated on some sections of the test. There were significant differences between these two groups on tense formation, subject-verb concord, plurals and possessives, but not on suffixing structural markers, zero copulas and other features which affect word order and the assigning of words to different form classes. Goodman has argued that the features in the first category do not hamper the reading process or interfere with understanding in any way. The second category, however, comes into play not in the initial stages of reading but at a later point when children are processing larger stretches of language and, as a result, neither Goodman nor Wight gives them any consideration. It is interesting, therefore, to note that no significant differences emerged between the two groups on features such as these, and this may go some way towards explaining why even West Indian children born in this country tend to underperform on comprehension tasks.

The finding that linguistic interference may well play a part in West Indian underperformance does not in any way, however, detract from the part which the school may be playing in this process. The implications of insensitive teacher behaviour on the reading achievement of West Indian children are so serious that they deserve special attention. Labov and Robins (1972) have pointed to the relationship between peer group status and reading failure. Out of a sample of forty-six boys who were members of street gangs no one was reading ahead of grade and only one was reading on grade. Yet out of a sample of thirty-two boys identified as non-members of street culture several were on grade and some were even ahead of grade. They suggest that culture conflict is a strong factor in reading failure. It seems almost inevitable that one of the consequences of being told that nearly everything you say is wrong is to reject the values of the teacher – and this includes learning to read – rather than to adopt forms which seem alien.

The school environment and school values are plainly not influencing the boys firmly grounded in street culture.... Teachers in city schools have little ability to reward or punish members of the street culture or to motivate learning by any means.

A teacher who constantly 'corrects' dialect features in a child's reading is harming the child in two ways. First, he is communicating that he finds the child's dialect unacceptable and, as we shall discuss at greater length in Chapter 5, the child is likely to interpret this to mean that he himself is unacceptable. If he is rejected by the teacher in this way he, in his turn, is likely to reject the teacher and all he stands for. Second, the teacher who corrects dialect features in early reading is encouraging the child to be a word caller and not to read for meaning. He is failing to recognize that the child is using his linguistic competence to translate and discover meaning from the passage; and he is being instrumental in destroying essential strategies for successful reading at more advanced stages. Goodman sums this up:

In encouraging divergent speakers to use their language competence, both receptive and productive, and accepting their dialect based miscues, we minimize the effect of dialect differences. In rejecting their dialects we maximize the effect.

How much 'interference'?

A survey of the areas of potential interference shows that children influenced by Creole may often be at a considerable disadvantage when they are educated through the medium of standard English. There are two kinds of difficulty: problems of comprehension and problems of production. Listening comprehension is most difficult on first contact with the school, whereas reading comprehension seems to become a more serious problem as the passages get progressively more difficult and further removed from Creole. Problems in producing standard English can also be persistent and, although interference is more marked in the early stages, many Creole features can be detected in the children's speech and writing throughout the age range. It is possible to argue in this case, however, that the main obstacle to educational success is not the language differences themselves but people's attitudes towards these differences.

It is impossible to estimate the proportion of West Indian children who find themselves at a disadvantage because of their different linguistic background. There may well be many children who are completely bidialectal, and many who are sufficiently bidialectal for Creole interference not to constitute a major educational problem. But, by the same token, there are also many children who show evidence of considerable linguistic interference and whose language difficulties are aggravated or, at least, perpetuated by teachers who either do not understand or are unsympathetic towards their special problems. It is very important, therefore, that teachers should appreciate the nature of the differences between Creole and standard English, so that they can predict areas of difficulty. It is equally important that they should be fully aware of the impact which insensitive handling of the situation may have on the children.

Chapter 5

Language attitudes and educational success

Up to the present we have considered some of the most common misconceptions about Creole and other non-standard speech, but we have not discussed in any depth the implications of these misconceptions. This is a serious omission inasmuch as there is a good deal of evidence that attitudes towards a language and attitudes towards speakers of that language are closely related. As we have already pointed out, the socially powerful are almost invariably felt to be well spoken, while the speech of the poor is universally stigmatized. It seems as if we lend a certain respectability to our disapproval of other people by channelling it into criticisms of the way they speak.

Whether criticism is directed explicitly at a group of people or implicitly at their speech, the consequences are likely to be the same. In an educational setting it may mean that the teacher has low expectations of the child's ability and, as we shall be discussing later in the chapter, low teacher expectation often leads to low pupil achievement. This, then, is a crucial area. To explore it further we need to understand the role of stereotyping behaviour in our reactions to both the language and the identity of other social groupings.

Stereotyping

Speech is one of the most important markers of social and ethnic boundaries. Even an untrained person has no difficulty in recognizing different kinds of speech and making judgments about the speaker. This does not necessarily mean that everyone can identify the exact geographical origins of a particular speaker with great accuracy. British listeners, for instance, quite often mistake a Canadian speaker for an American. But people can and, indeed, regularly do make generalizations on the basis of speech.

It is useful at this point to distinguish between accent and dialect. Accent refers only to pronunciation, whereas dialect involves both grammar and pronunciation. Thus a middle-class educated Welshman may use standard English grammar but speak with distinctly Welsh pronunciation. A working-class Welshman, on the other hand, will differ not only in pronunciation but also in grammar and here we are dealing with a difference of dialect. Very definite stereotypes grow up around different kinds of speech. Observations about a person's speech can thus be seen to be, more properly, observations about the person himself.

To understand this more clearly we need to look at the central part which stereotyping plays in all human behaviour. It can be seen as a very useful and necessary process which allows us to form comfortable social relationships within the norms of decorum of our culture. There is, however, the danger that typing might be exaggerated to the point of rigidity: it can be used as the justification for excluding ourselves from certain social relationships and for the subordination or rejection of particular individuals or groups of individuals.

It is possible to distinguish between two kinds of stereotype traits – actual cultural differences which attract attention simply because they are different, and negations of values held by the in-group which have little bearing on objective truth. An example of the first is the tendency of the West Indian child to smile when scolded. The British teacher is most likely to interpret this as insolence; a West Indian teacher knows that this is simply a sign of nervousness. On the other hand, the second kind of trait (for example, laziness, or childishness) is not specific to one culture, nor can it be proved to be objectively true. Unfortunately when any one stereotype trait is observed it tends to evoke the whole range of the stereotype.

The universality of the second kind of trait is quite striking. It concentrates on issues which threaten the order of the community and, thus, one frequently hears foreigners referred to as dirty, dishonest and aggressive; they have strange eating habits and stranger sexual practices. A rapid survey of history shows that these very traits were attributed to the Africans by the Greeks and Romans, to the Irish by the English and to the Lapps by the Scandinavians. To this we can no doubt add the characteristics sometimes associated with West Indians by the British.

Language attitudes as indicators of social attitudes

Such are the mechanisms of the stereotyping processes which determine our attitudes to particular groups and individuals who are members of these groups, It is very difficult, however, to establish with any certainty what precisely a person's attitudes are, since his answers are likely to be influenced by the impression he wishes to make on the questioner. One attempt at solving the problem has been through the study of language attitudes, since these almost invariably reflect more general attitudes towards the speaker. But this approach, too, poses certain difficulties and there are reports that although people often have very strong opinions about speech, very few can express exactly what they feel (see, for example, Labov, 1966, pp. 405–6).

Although direct questioning is of very limited value, another technique – the semantic differential – has proved very successful. Subjects are required to evaluate a person's speech along a seven point scale between two polar terms. For example,

good ⌐ ⌐ ⌐ ⌐ ⌐ ⌐ ⌐ bad

Although this is only an indirect measure, all the indications are that it enables one to arrive at a reliable picture of the stereotypes which one group holds of another, since the same profile of reactions emerges on repeated sampling.

Wallace Lambert and his associates in Montreal developed a very useful extension of the semantic differential, called the matched guise technique. Working with French and English

Canadians, Lambert *et al.* (1960) demonstrated the way in which the stereotypes which the majority group have about the minority systematically affect evaluations of speech. The taped speech of five bilinguals, speaking once in French and once in English, was played to both French and English 'judges'. They were asked to evaluate each speaker on a series of personality and physical traits on a scale from very little to very much. The judges were not aware that the same people spoke twice and it was thus possible to match their reactions to the two guises for each speaker. It was found that the English judges evaluated the English guises more favourably on most traits. But perhaps more surprising was the discovery that French judges also evaluated English guises more favourably and their evaluations of the French guises were even less complimentary than those of the English judges. Experiments carried out on a wide range of languages, dialects and accents have shown similar results.

Even when speech preferences are explained in terms of social structure, many people still feel that low-status speech *sounds* ugly. For this reason we need to give serious consideration to the question of whether aesthetic judgments are culturally conditioned or absolute. There is certainly no doubt that rural dialects like Somerset or Highland Scots are felt to be more attractive than urban dialects like Cockney or Birmingham. But this is far more likely to be due to our nostalgic attachment to the countryside over the city than to any inherent quality. This is a hypothesis which can easily be tested by asking any foreign visitor to evaluate different British accents. Even English-speaking Americans have no definite pattern of preference and often find it difficult to differentiate between various accents, let alone state a preference (cf. Trudgill and Giles, forthcoming). Similarly, when British judges have been asked to evaluate different dialects of French or Greek, they have failed to identify the high-status variety. There would seem to be no basis, then, for claims of aesthetic superiority of one variety over another.

But this tells us nothing of how the relationship between dialect differences and attitudes towards dialect differences actually works. One of the most influential workers in this field is William Labov, and one of his special interests has been critical linguistic variables which invoke stereotyped attitudes. In one study he examined in great detail the presence or absence of /r/ in the final position in a word or before a consonant (e.g. *car, cart*). He found that all informants in an area of New York City between the ages of eighteen and thirty-nine recognized the presence of /r/ as socially preferred as did 66 per cent of those over forty. Presumably the older group were less sensitive to this variable because when they were growing up the pronunciation without the /r/ was the norm. Informants below the age of twenty were also less reliable in identifying this feature, probably because they were not yet fully attuned to the socially significant dialect features of their community.

Labov makes use of two main techniques in eliciting the attitudes to speech which explain his findings. The first is a subjective reaction test which consists of the same speaker reading sentences which differ mainly in one linguistic variable. Subjects are then asked to evaluate the speaker according to certain occupational categories: 'What is the highest job the speaker could hold speaking as he does?'; according to a scale of toughness — 'If the speaker was in a street fight how likely would he be to come out on top?'; and according to a friend-ship scale — 'If you knew the speaker for a long time how likely would he be to become a good friend of yours?' Over the whole sample there was an inverse relationship between the job and toughness scale; but the friendship scale followed the job scale in the case of the three upper social classes and the fight scale for the lower-working-class group.

The second technique involves self-evaluation. When asked which of several forms is a feature of their own speech people generally choose the prestige form rather than the one they actually use. Labov proposes that this behaviour is an indi-cation of 'pressures from above' while the non-prestige form continues to be used because of the need to identify with a particular sub-group, as a result of 'pressures from below'. This is clearly seen in the pattern of preference in the friend-ship scale which emerges for the lower-working-class group. The mechanics of linguistic stereotyping are thus complex, but none the less possible to detect and describe.

Williams (1973) has gone a step further in an attempt to link the critical features of the kind isolated by Labov with the wider range of stereotypes associated with the work of

Lambert. He proposes two potentially independent dimensions – confidence/eagerness and ethnicity/non-standardness – to account for ratings of a child's social status, and found that these judgmental dimensions could be readily predicted on the basis of selected linguistic features. Thus, incidence of silent pausing was inversely related to ratings of confidence/eagerness, and non-standard forms were related to ethnicity/non-standardness.

There are two ways in which listeners can react to this two-dimensional model. Either they can respond to the speaker's social stereotype, which would result in a gross classification across the two dimensions, or they can base their evaluations on individual characteristics of the speaker which would allow independent ratings on the two dimensions. The subjects in the Williams experiments seem to have taken the former course.

How, then, do these findings relate to West Indians in Britain? There are certainly indications that group identity is very important for West Indian adolescents in this country. There are even reports from teachers that some youths who apparently had no features of Creole speech in primary school have started speaking with noticeable West Indian accents in secondary school, and it is well documented that the use of Creole in peer-group conversation is widespread. Hebdige (1976), for instance, comments on the ways in which West Indian youths have developed Creole as a symbol of group identity:

> Language is used [by members of certain West Indian sub-cultures] as a particularly effective way of resisting assimilation and preventing infiltration by members of the dominant groups. As a screening device it has proved to be invaluable; and the 'Bongo talk' and patois of the Rude Boy deliberately emphasize its subversive rhythms so that it becomes an aggressive assertion of racial and class identities. As a living index of the extent of the black's alienation from the cultural norms and goals of those who occupy high positions in the social structure the Creole language is unique.

This has serious implications for the educational performance of West Indians. One's ability to speak a language –

whether it be French or standard English — depends not only on exposure or ability but on a person's desire to identify with another group. If West Indians feel alienated from British society and consider that they have little or no chance of attaining a particular goal — like a good job or social acceptance — then they are not likely to be motivated to learn the speech patterns associated with those members of society who have attained such goals.

The position of West Indians in British society is very depressing. We have already seen that there is extensive unemployment and an unmistakable pattern of underperformance in schools. The very poor state of relations between Black youths and the police is a further reflection of their alienation from British society. It would thus seem logical, in view of the research findings reviewed above, that West Indian speech would be stigmatized and held in very low esteem by the indigenous White population, and that the Black community would be acutely aware of this stigmatization. Those who identify with British culture will show few Creole features in their speech; those who reject British society will show marked Creole features.

There is very little empirical evidence on attitudes towards West Indian speech, but the one study which has been undertaken in this field (Edwards, 1978a) confirms that both British and West Indian judges view West Indian speech very negatively. Four groups were considered to be of main importance: teachers, West Indian children and their working- and middleclass peers.

Four children, all in their first year at secondary school, were recorded. The first was a Barbadian girl who was born in Britain and was completely bidialectal. She spoke once with the working-class Reading accent which she habitually uses at school and at a later point in a West Indian accent characterized by many phonological features of Creole, though not a great number of grammatical features. The result was a sample of speech which was recognizably West Indian but none the less readily understandable to a speaker of British English. The other children were an English boy who had a working-class Reading accent, a professor's son who spoke with 'Received Pronunciation' and a recently arrived Jamaican girl who spoke with very marked phonological and grammatical features of Creole, barely intelligible to a British listener. All spoke fluently for thirty seconds on the subject of going to the dentist.

Using the semantic differential technique, two sets of scales were built into a questionnaire. The first set related to the children's speech and was based largely on the scales used in the Detroit study (Wolfram, 1969):

The second group of scales relates to the child's behaviour and was based on categories suggested by the Bristol Social Adjustment Guide (Stott, 1971). The following scales were used:

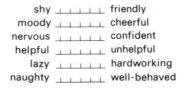

Two questions were added to the end of the questionnaire. The first dealt with potential academic ability. Subjects were required to answer,

> How far do you think this child will get in school?
> C.S.E. / O levels / A levels

The second question,

> Do you think this child would be interesting to have in the class?   Yes / No

was included mainly to assess the attitudes of the school children, since it was assumed that teachers would feel bound to answer positively.

Teacher attitudes towards speech

Because of the effect which teacher attitudes may well have on West Indian behaviour, this is obviously an important group to consider. There are, however, certain practical difficulties in establishing how British teachers feel towards West Indian children. Attitudes towards educational researchers can vary from extreme hostility to full co-operation, and since only those well disposed towards the tester and his stated aims would be likely to agree to take part, there would be great difficulty in ensuring a balanced sample. There are also problems in administering tests, since teachers are seldom together long enough in school hours and it is often difficult to stay behind afterwards.

An attractive alternative was to work with student teachers. Testing could take place in a lecture period, as this offered a reasonably sized group who were in one place long enough to take the test. Another point in their favour was that since they were not fully involved in teaching they would be less likely to interpret the experiment as a threat to their personal values and practices. In the more academic atmosphere of a college of education it was also easier to disguise the actual aim of the test, namely to establish how the subjects felt about West Indian children and their language. Objections, admittedly, might be raised against the validity of using a student sample to reflect teacher opinion. It is commonly held that there is no substitute for actual classroom experience and that much of the educational theory learned in training is never actually applied. Even so, difficulties in ensuring a balanced cross-section of teacher opinion and the practical benefits of using students as subjects were felt to outweigh these disadvantages.

A group of twenty final-year students was approached and asked if they were prepared to take part in an experiment to find out how accurate people could be in assessing personality on the basis of a small sample of speech. They were told that the recordings had been made some years previously and that now full profiles on each child were available.

Results showed unmistakable signs of stereotyping behaviour. The 'judges' found no significant differences between the two working-class speakers, nor between the West Indian girls; but highly significant differences emerged between their evaluations of the middle-class boy and the working-class speaker and between the working-class children and the West Indian girls. The student teachers were almost unanimous in their order of preference: middle-class speech, working-class speech, West Indian speech. The same pattern was found in their evaluations of behaviour − the middle-class boy was considered most favourably, followed by the working-class boy and the Barbadian girl speaking with a working-class accent and then the West Indian girl and the Barbadian girl speaking with a West Indian accent. It would seem that the social stereotype associated with a particular kind of speech evokes a gross classification and that little attention is paid to detail. But the most striking feature of this study is that the same girl was judged more favourably when speaking with a working-class English accent than with a West Indian accent.

Two other factors were considered: the relative academic potential of the children and their desirability as members of a class. These results were largely consistent with the previous ones. The middle-class boy was felt to have the highest potential and the working guise is viewed more favourably than the West Indian. The teachers' evaluation of the children's desirability as members of a class is, however, surprising. It had been hypothesized that there would be no significant differences in their appraisals of the speakers in this respect, in view of the emphasis of modern educational philosophy on children as individuals. It would seem that this philosophy has had some impact since working-class children are not considered less desirable than their middle-class peers. Its influence, however, does not seem to have been sufficient to overcome their negative feelings about West Indian children or, at least, children whose speech is recognizably West Indian.

Testing British children's attitudes towards speech

There can be little doubt that the teachers who took part in the testing described above were behaving in accordance with widely held social stereotypes of the speakers. The prevalence of these stereotypes is largely confirmed by results of the same experiment which was repeated with other British groups. Samples of twenty working-class children from a large Reading comprehensive school and twenty middle-class children, half of whom came from a girls' grammar school and half from a direct grant school for boys, were approached and asked to take part in testing. Their average age was fourteen, and since there are reports that children as young as twelve perform quite satisfactorily on this kind of evaluative task (see Shuy, 1970, p. 184), it was considered that the tasks would be well within their capability. These children, then, were asked to build up a picture of the speakers in the recordings 'in the same way as you would when hearing someone you had never met in a phone conversation'.

Results showed that both middle- and working-class judges agree with the student teachers in assigning high status to the middle-class boy, both in speech and behaviour. There is an interesting departure, however, in their evaluations of the working class and West Indian guises. The working-class judges follow the student teachers and view the West Indian guise less favourably. The middle-class judges, on the other hand, do not distinguish between the two guises. At first sight it might seem that the middle-class children are departing from the stereotyping behaviour of the other groups, but this interpretation seems unfounded. They still agree that the middle-class boy has highest status, and fail to distinguish between either the working-class speakers or the West Indian girls. It would seem, therefore, that the middle-class children, too, are influenced by social stereotypes and that they simply look upon working-class and West Indian speakers equally unfavourably.

A similar pattern emerges in the children's evaluations of academic potential. Both groups of judges agreed that the middle-class boy has greatest academic potential, but neither group distinguishes between working-class and West Indian guises. It can be argued that, to a large extent, these results reflect educational reality, but they do none the less present still further evidence of social stereotyping.

A somewhat different pattern emerges in the children's evaluations of the speaker's desirability as a member of the class, and only the middle-class judges feel that the middle-class boy would be an interesting class mate. It would seem that, even though the working-class judges recognize his status in general terms, they are not prepared to extend this to more personal considerations. This, of course, is a pattern which has already been established in the work of Labov (1966), where working-class friendship preferences were related to a scale of toughness.

Thus we see that several different British groups evaluate speech according to their social stereotypes and that there is a high degree of agreement, especially amongst the teachers and working-class children. These groups will in fact be the ones who have greatest contact with West Indians, and the middle-class tendency to group West Indian and working-class speakers together perhaps reflects a lack of firsthand experience. It emerges, then, that teachers are more likely to be representative of British society as a whole rather than a group particularly prone to making rigid generalizations.

Testing West Indians' attitudes towards speech

West Indians' appraisal of their own speech is obviously of critical importance to their linguistic and social behaviour. It was decided, therefore, to test a group of West Indian children from the same school as the working-class children described above. Before testing it was extremely difficult to predict what the results would be. There are many indications that West Indians are becoming increasingly alienated from British society, and are responding by developing their own Black youth culture. But it was impossible to assess whether recent assertions of group identity and solidarity would be reflected in heightened confidence and self-concept or in a sense of insecurity, characteristic of minority groups described by Lambert and others.

An analysis of the results showed that the West Indian judges agreed with both student teacher and child judges that the middle-class boy had highest status in terms of both speech and behaviour. A certain ambivalence, however, could be detected in their evaluations of the West Indian and working-class guises. Although they showed no marked preference for either guise in their evaluations of speech, the working-class guise was rated more favourably on behaviour.

West Indian judgments of academic potential and desirability as a member of the class corresponded most closely to those of the middle-class children. They, too, assigned highest status to the middle-class boy, whom they considered had the greatest academic potential and would be the most interesting member of the class. But there was no evidence of any preference for the West Indian speakers, which suggests that feelings of group solidarity do not strongly influence their evaluations. West Indian children have clearly internalized the stereotypes of the dominant White society; like all minority groups studied to date, they undervalue the speech and speakers of their own group.

The role of teacher expectation

The evidence suggests that West Indian speech is socially stigmatized and that this in turn is a reflection of the low position of West Indians in society. The extent of stereotyping revealed in the research reported above has serious implications for the educational performance of West Indian children. Attitudes provide a frame of reference so that all a person does, sees or thinks will be consistent with this frame of reference. They provide an indication of how we are likely to act providing we are free to do so, in relation to a person, object or situation. Although it is not possible to predict with any degree of certainty that the student teachers included in the testing which we have been discussing will behave in a way which discriminates between different groups of pupils, we cannot overlook the possibility that this may be the case. Nor can we overlook the possibility that feedback from the teacher will adversely affect the child's motivation and ability to learn.

There is a considerable body of research relating to teachers' attitudes which suggests that teachers' expectations play an important part in the level of pupil performance. Perhaps the most frequently quoted work in this field is *Pygmalion in the Classroom* (Rosenthal and Jakobson, 1968). Their research was carried out in an American elementary school situated in a working-class area. It was divided into three streams according to reading ability and there was a disproportionately high number of Mexicans in the lowest stream. Children were pre-tested with a standard non-verbal test of intelligence which teachers were led to believe would predict 'intellectual blooming'. A list of 20 per cent of the children, randomly selected, who would show sudden intellectual growth was then presented to the teachers. After the first year of the experiment, a significant expectancy advantage was found particularly among the first- and second-year children. In the next year younger children lost their advantage, though older children increased theirs. Since they had changed teacher, the younger children may have required continued contact with the 'influencer' to keep up the change in their behaviour. Older children, on the other hand, may have been able to maintain the change autonomously.

This study has in fact been criticized by both Thorndike (1968) and Snow (1969). Significantly, though, the object of their criticism is the inadequacy of the research procedures, and the inappropriateness of their conclusions rather than the basic hypothesis. There will, for instance, always be difficult-ies in experimental design when dealing with classroom situ-ations which involve small numbers of children. In addition to this, unless the information given to the teachers is grossly false — in which case it is unlikely to be believed — the study will probably not produce statistically significant results. However, evidence from other sources (reviewed, for example, by Pidgeon, 1970; Verma and Bagley, 1975) lends support to the general conclusion that pupil performance is influenced by factors in school organization, including teacher-pupil interaction. There are strong indications that many teachers perceive poor and ethnic minority children in a different light and that this in turn leads to different treat-ment and teaching techniques which work to the detriment of the children.

Investigations of linguistic behaviour in the classroom also support the notion of 'self-fulfilling prophecies'. Frender, Brown and Lambert (1970), for instance, considered the relationship between speech characteristics and educational success. They found that those lower-class pupils who were doing well in school had a distinctly different speech style from those who were underattaining. They concluded that 'how a child presents himself through speech ... may very well influence teachers' opinions and evaluation of him.'

Williams, Whitehead and Miller (1971) found that teachers were prepared to rate not only speech samples but stereotyped descriptions of the kind:

He is a Mexican-American boy who comes from a family of ten. His father is a gas station attendant. He lives in a lower class neighbourhood.

Seligman, Tucker and Lambert (1972) used combinations of good drawings and compositions with poor or good voices, based on the previous evaluations of student teacher judges, to build up profiles of eight hypothetical third-grade boys. These were presented to a new set of student teacher judges. The results showed that subjects considered voice when judging intelligence and both voice and physical appearance in judging student capability.

It would seem then that speech types serve as identifiers which evoke stereotypes held by ourselves and others. Since we tend to behave according to these stereotypes, we thereby translate our attitudes into social reality. The implications of the negative feelings of the student teachers towards West Indian children (described above) are thus far-reaching. The way in which teachers' attitudes affect children's performance is uncertain. It may be that, deliberately or unintentionally, they undervalue the work of children that they feel uncomfortable about. Or it may be that children who sense this personal devaluation become so insecure that they cannot perform efficiently. Whatever the mechanisms involved, the danger remains that children may underachieve as a result of teachers' attitudes towards them and their language.

Language attitudes and educational performance

The interrelationship between language differences and attitudes to these differences can now be seen to be a highly complex one. The teacher who does not or is not prepared to recognize the problems of the Creole-speaking child in a British English situation can only conclude that he is stupid when he gives either an inappropriate response or no response at all. The stereotyping process leads features of Creole to be stigmatized and to develop connotations of, amongst other things, low academic ability. The teacher is then more likely to allow the stereotype to determine her behaviour towards the child, and low teacher expectation will very probably lead to low pupil performance. The child, for his part, feels threatened, especially in the early stages, by comprehension difficulties. These and the teacher's behaviour towards him produce a state of linguistic insecurity and he is very likely to seem inarticulate as a result. This reinforces the teacher's preconceived ideas and so the cycle is perpetuated.

Chapter 6

Practical approaches to language

What can the teacher do?

Having discussed the structure of Creole and the special problems which children influenced by Creole face in the British school system, the question remains as to what practical course of action teachers should take. The situation presented by large numbers of children from different language backgrounds is a fairly new one for British schools, and requires a considerable degree of innovation and adaptation. Often the presence of West Indian children has drawn attention to wider issues which are also of concern to indigenous children; sometimes problems are peculiar to West Indian children. In either case, the arrival of children from different linguistic and cultural backgrounds has given teachers the opportunity to reappraise the content, philosophy and processes of the education they are providing, and the benefits of such a reappraisal will certainly be felt by immigrant and non-immigrant alike.

The problems of dialect speakers are not new to British teachers. Geordie, Glasgow, Rhondda and Somerset schools have always been faced with the dilemma that, although standard English is expected to be the language of education, the vast majority of the children they teach are non-standard speakers. The arrival of West Indian children, however, created a more difficult situation. Not only was their dialect further removed from standard English than regional English dialects, but it was outside the range of experience of most British teachers and almost totally unfamiliar.

99

The only country with problems of a similar nature and proportion is the USA. Black Americans speak a dialect (Black English Vernacular or BEV) very similar to Creole, although not as far removed from standard English, and they have much in common with West Indians in Britain. Both form substantial minority groups with a language and culture sufficiently different from mainstream language and culture for educators to feel that this constitutes a problem. It is valuable, therefore, to consider the ways in which education-alists have approached the American situation and to assess the relevance of their findings for the teaching of British dialect speakers in general and West Indians in particular.

Dialect eradication

For many years the dominant trend in teaching Black Americans was to try to eradicate their dialect. The motiv-ation for this approach has changed from time to time. Initially, there was a strong feeling that BEV was an illogical mode of expression which did not provide an adequate basis for abstract thought. Linguists like Labov (1972a), however, have shown the faulty premises on which these assumptions were based, and it is now generally agreed that all languages and dialects are regular, rule-governed systems, equally ex-pressive and equally capable of fulfilling all the communi-cation needs of their speakers. A later, and more laudable, motive for eradicating dialect was that the standard language is essential for educational success and that dialect speakers must abandon their original speech patterns if they are to be socially mobile.

The American experience has shown, however, that, regard-less of motive, dialect eradication simply does not work. It is not difficult to understand why this should be the case. We have already reviewed research which strongly suggests that constant correction of dialect speakers (and this is what dialect eradication involves) is harmful in two distinct ways. As we have shown in Chapter 5, if we belittle an accent or dialect we, for our part, are making a covert statement about our perceptions of people who speak in this way. Because of the strong links between language and identity, the child, for his part, will perceive any remarks about the way he speaks as directed against him personally. The consequences in the early stages of school may be particularly worrying. Young children tend to look upon their teacher as a kind of parent substitute (cf. Torrey, 1973) and teachers make use of this attitude in motivating children to learn. If, however, the teacher cannot accept the child – and his ways – for what they are, there is no basis for any parent–child relationship. The child is far more likely to reject the teacher and the values of the school than to conform to strange and unfriendly practices, and the teacher may well be preparing the way for years of hostility and alienation.

Second, attempts at dialect eradication can lead to confusion and lack of confidence. If we take first the case of writing, it is clear that the teacher who hopes to eradicate dialect features from the written work of West Indian children requires great persistence. If, for instance, she is trying to teach a child that -*s* must be added to all plural nouns, or that -*ed* must be added to all past-tense verbs, then it means that *all* dialect forms must be 'corrected'. A survey of marking methods shows that this is not common practice. In most cases a token -*s* or -*ed* is added to a few forms in each piece of work, while many others are left unchanged. It has already been shown, however, that past-tense and plural markers do appear in the written work of West Indian children at least some of the time, and that they base their decision on whether to use standard or non-standard forms on considerations of formality, subject matter, etc. The haphazard correction of Creole forms is therefore hardly likely to be effective in communicating that this is an 'all or nothing' affair for the standard speaker.

Of course, teachers do not correct consistently for very good reason. The page would be so covered with marks from a red felt-tip pen that there would be a very serious threat to self-confidence. On the other hand, selective correction, especially in the early stages, can only lead to confusion. The extensive overgeneralization and hypercorrection reported in Chapter 4 can leave us in little doubt that this will be the case.

By the same token, correction of dialect-based miscues in reading can have a very undesirable effect. It discourages children from using their linguistic competence in predicting and drawing meaning from what they are reading, so that they read instead for accuracy and show very little understanding of the material they are working with. Even when the teacher is using an exclusively phonic method, the special difficulties of West Indian children who are constantly 'corrected' are clear to see. Labov (1969) points out that:

> Eventually the child may stop trying to identify the shapes of letters that follow the vowel, and guess wildly at each word after he deciphers the first few letters. Or he may lose confidence in the alphabetic principle as a whole. The loss of confidence seems to occur frequently in the third and fourth grades [nine- and ten-year-olds] and it is a characteristic of many children who are effectively non-readers.

Years of attempts at dialect eradication in America have thus shown that, apart from ethical considerations, this approach is both ineffective in achieving its aims and poses a serious threat to the confidence of non-standard speakers.

The bidialectal approach

An American alternative to dialect eradication has been the bidialectal approach. Instead of denigrating the dialect, the differences between the dialect and the standard are discussed openly and the child learns to convert his own speech patterns into standard forms, often by specific teaching strategies, including language drills. Bidialectalism, unlike dialect eradication, is aimed at helping the child to produce standard English in his written work and not in his speech. It is recognized that any attempt to change speech patterns must come from the child himself, and that any move on the part of the teacher is likely to provoke a hostile response. It is very important that the child is not made to feel that his dialect is in any way inadequate, and, because efforts are restricted to written work, the chances of alienating the child are far smaller with this method than with the dialect eradication approach.

An important discussion developed in the 1960s and early 1970s amongst advocates of bidialectalism about the need for dialect materials in early reading. Writers like Baratz (1969a; 1969b) felt strongly that literacy should be based on the child's actual language and not the language which he is assumed to speak. She saw a programme using dialect readers as having several advantages, including success in teaching the ghetto child to read, the support to the self-image and being able to demonstrate where standard English and dialect differ and coincide.

This movement has, however, met with considerable opposition. Basing special materials on a non-prestigious dialect has met with a great deal of resentment from the dialect speakers themselves, who have interpreted this as yet another attempt to deny them access to standard English and its attendant social mobility. There has also been opposition to dialect readers on linguistic grounds. Writers like Goodman and Buck (1973) and Liu (1976) challenge the assumption that reading failure is due to structural differences between dialect and standard and therefore question whether the use of dialect readers would be of particular advantage over materials written in standard English.

But, although the need for early readers in dialect is open to question, a great deal can be said for the use of dialect at other stages. The teacher who simply pays lip service to the value of different dialects is hardly likely to gain credibility. It is only by treating dialect as a serious object of study that the child is likely to believe the teacher's claim that both standard and non-standard language have their own intrinsic worth.

Any attempts at systematically teaching standard English, however, must be reserved for the later stages of education, where literacy based on the child's own linguistic competence is firmly established. This does not necessarily mean that 'anything goes'. All children, regardless of their social or linguistic backgrounds, make mistakes and need guidance. They often make organizational errors or fail to present an argument coherently. They also make mistakes related to their language development which have nothing to do with dialect and misuse words and constructions that they do not fully understand. The girl who used 'euthanasia' to mean 'birth control' throughout an essay on world population did not do so because of dialect differences. Similarly, children will make mistakes of presentation – spelling, punctuation, paragraphing. These are features of another medium, the written medium, and are essential if the child, or another person, is to be able to read back what is written.

As far as dialect features are concerned there is no evidence from research in linguistics or reading that these hamper the early stages of literacy. In fact, the evidence we have suggests that the only disadvantage is the school-imposed one resulting from rejection of the child's dialect. A bidialectal approach would therefore allow children to use their own dialect in speech, reading and writing in the early years of school without any intervention from the teacher. Only when reading and writing in the child's own dialect was firmly established would the teacher draw the child's attention to differences, and the advantages of learning to write standard English be pointed out.

Of the two approaches, dialect eradication and bidialectalism, the latter would seem to be the more ethically acceptable and also the one more likely to succeed. There are likely to be difficulties, however, even with this approach. Its success is dependent on the West Indian's early experience of school. If attitudes towards the child's use of Creole in the first school have been prescriptive, and if his confidence has already been undermined, the amount which can be achieved with the bidialectal approach is limited, no matter how sympathetically teachers may present the case. Even allowing for goodwill at all stages the child may be more readily convinced by the attitudes outside the school than by those inside. The influence of society on a child's willingness and ability to learn cannot be overestimated. Le Page (1974) formulates this problem in the following terms:

> Learning must now be seen as, to a large extent, a socially determined process. One's ability to learn to change the rules for one's behaviour is constrained by one's motivation to do so, one's motivation to do so is constrained by feedback from society as to the chances of attaining a particular goal.

The West Indian child with older brothers and sisters who have underperformed in school, and who may well be unemployed, may prefer to believe his own family experience that social mobility through education is unattainable rather than the exhortations of his teacher that the acquisition of standard English is the passport to educational success. But despite the note of pessimism, bidialectalism seems the most realistic and practical course to follow. It is certainly more attainable than the final approach which some writers have advocated: dialect appreciation.

Dialect appreciation

It is established fact that no language or dialect is superior to another and, so the argument goes, different dialects should not have different status in schools. Although linguistically this stance is perfectly acceptable, and should certainly be accepted as a long-term aim, such is the strength of tradition surrounding the use of standard English that it is highly unlikely that dialects should be given equal status, at least in the foreseeable future.

There are enormous difficulties in persuading teachers to treat all dialects alike. The range of opinions on language within a single school, or even a single department, is such that the idea of pursuing a policy of dialect appreciation becomes Utopian. Even if this were not the case, we have to think of the consequences for the children. Crystal (1976) explains potential dangers in these terms (p. 71):

> The children being taught now are going to have to grow up in a society where the formal standard language and its various varieties retains considerable prestige. Its practitioners still, in several walks of life, call the tune ... We may wish to change society to remove some of the stigma that attaches to certain language forms. But it seems unreasonable to expect the child to do it for us, and unfair to give him the impression that anything goes, as long as it is 'sincere and expressive', when we know full well that in real life there are other linguistic standards which educated people are expected to live up to.

It is true that in many ways it is easier to achieve attitude change in teachers than to change the speech of dialect speakers, but this will be such a lengthy process that some more practical course must be followed in the meantime.

105

Suitability of reading schemes

Any teacher who accepts the implications of the findings reviewed so far must recognize the importance of being able to discriminate between dialect based 'errors' and genuine mistakes. Initially, this is essential if we wish to avoid 'correcting' features which are perfectly regular within the child's own linguistic system; later it is essential if we wish to explain systematically the differences between Creole and the standard. This is important no matter what materials the school is using, but two methods – the 'initial teaching alphabet' (i.t.a.) and *Breakthrough to literacy* – require special mention.

As we have shown in Chapter 2, the sound system of Creole is quite different from that of standard English. Many of the i.t.a. symbols represent sounds which do not regularly appear in the speech of West Indian children, and therefore the West Indian using these materials would have no greater advantage than if he were using traditional orthography. As far as writing is concerned, the West Indian sound system can easily be constructed using the i.t.a. symbols, as examples from children's writing listed below clearly show.

wons apon a tiem ʃhær woʒ a little boi hω liv *wid* (with) hiʒ muʃher (Paul, 6)

ʃhen wεε went hæm and wεε hav *tos* (toast) and tεε (Christopher, 6)

he *bod* (bird) woʒ very nies (Paula, 6)

It could be argued that this system might be a useful aid to literacy. But this would depend very much on the teacher being familiar with the child's sound system and consequently able to discriminate between dialect spellings and genuine mistakes. Multiracial schools using i.t.a. need to think very seriously about its implications for West Indian children. Few teachers are sufficiently familiar with Creole phonology – and inter-island differences – to be able to use the system confident that they are supporting the child's own dialect and not accepting a mistake.

The same provisos apply, of course, to the word building activities of *Breakthrough to literacy*, or any other phonic approach. The sentence-making activities of *Breakthrough*, however, are ideal for use with dialect speakers. Each child has a folder containing frequently occurring words printed on card inserts, and blank cards for the teacher to write words chosen by the child. He can then build up sentences, which he later transfers to a book, by placing words from the folder in a stand. Writing goes hand in hand with reading and both are based on the child's own experience of life and language. In this way there need be no conflict between the dialect and the standard and many of the disadvantages of other approaches to literacy can be by-passed altogether.

There is, however, one danger which should be noted. Teachers risk undoing all the good work which can be achieved with this method by translating dialect features into standard English, either when reading the child's work or when writing it down. In doing this, they are falling into the same trap as those who wish to eradicate dialect, and there is no reason to suppose that they will be any more successful.

Problems of implementation

The difficulties of implementing even the more modest bi-dialectal approach are enormous. Traditional views towards Creole and all non-standard speech are so deeply entrenched that the process of change is likely to be a lengthy one. The controversy caused by the Language Arts Syllabus published by the Trinidad and Tobago Ministry of Education and Culture (1975) and discussed by Carrington and Borely (1977) is a good example of the kind of problems which are involved. The new syllabus challenges the traditional assumption that Creole is slovenly and unacceptable, and suggests that, since this is the only means of communication available to children on entering school, they should be allowed to express themselves in Creole in the early years. It is argued that this atmosphere of acceptance, together with a more structured approach towards the teaching of standard English, is more likely to result in success than the censorious and *ad hoc* teaching methods of the past.

The publication of the syllabus provoked an outraged response from an important sector of the community, and, as Carrington and Borely (1977) make clear, a heated debate ensued in the Trinidad press for some time. Often there was confusion over what had actually been proposed. An anonymous correspondent, for instance, suggests:

> To carry this thing to its logical conclusion: if the language of the barrack yard and the market place is to be the accepted mode of expression in the school-room, in the office and in life generally, all books would be useless, there would be nothing for our children to learn and we could well close the schools and universities, save the high wages of these experts and set them free to go and plant peas and gather nutmegs where they could give full play to this dialect stuff.

But there was also a failure to understand, or accept, that Creole was a perfectly valid linguistic system. Writers referred to it variously in terms of 'careless and sloppy speech', 'substandard intrusions' and the 'appalling use of language'. One contributor, Bowen, sums up the feelings of a large proportion of the West Indian population thus:

> Right here I may say that I contest strongly the claim that what the child speaks in his home is not English but the vernacular. In my view it is a form of English but very bad English.

As we have seen in Chapters 2 and 3, such comments bear no relationship to objective truth, but they do demonstrate how extremely sensitive we can be about language.

As in the West Indies, there has been some progress in promoting more favourable attitudes towards Creole in English schools. The Inner London Education Authority (ILEA), for instance, has undertaken a radical reappraisal of its policies for multiracial education, bringing it into line with the European Economic Community (EEC) directive which obliges governments 'to promote, in co-ordination with normal education, teaching of the mother tongue and culture of the country of origin.' Although in the case of West Indian children this would not involve the teaching of Creole, an attempt is being made to develop greater understanding of their language on the part of teachers, and to encourage the use of Creole in drama and poetry. It is interesting to note that these proposals provoked the same kind of response as the suggested curriculum reform in Trinidad. The headmaster of one London comprehensive school with a large proportion of West Indian pupils commented in the *Sunday Times* (16 October 1977) in no uncertain terms:

> Should I create a black curriculum? Should I put creole on the timetable? Over my dead body and the majority of my parents would cheer me to the skies. They want their children to get jobs. I will not even allow patois plays in the school. It must not be elevated to linguistic status at the expense of English.

It is also interesting that, like those who contributed to the *Trinidad Guardian*, this headmaster has misunderstood the aims of the new curriculum. There is, in fact, no suggestion that Creole should replace standard English; simply that a recognition of the child's own language and culture is likely to have a favourable effect on his attitudes to school and his progress in learning. The strength of prejudice against Creole however, as this comment shows, should not be underestimated.

Specialists or class teachers?

The question remains as to whether language should be the responsibility of specialist teachers or all teachers. A small number of local authorities, for instance, supply special help for children of West Indian origin. The oldest and best-established of these is the Waltham Forest Supplementary Service. Teachers work in a number of different schools in the Borough, withdrawing small groups of children to a special base in each school. Ealing operates along similar lines, but in addition to withdrawing groups of children, teachers work alongside class and subject teachers either by giving help to individual pupils or by assisting in team teaching.

Several other authorities make provision for special help on an *ad hoc* basis. Sometimes one or two teachers are made available on a part time basis to schools where there is a large proportion of West Indian children. This kind of provision is obviously less satisfactory than the more ambitious services provided by Waltham Forest and Ealing. With less manpower and less expertise, it is obviously more difficult to assess where the most urgent need lies. There are fewer resources and there can be little exchange of ideas and resources.

There are also fundamental objections to this kind of service, whether on a limited or a more ambitious scale. In the same way that Black American parents objected to early readers in dialect, many West Indian parents and children are suspicious of anything which isolates them from their English peers. Especially after the experience of ESN schools, 'special classes' are often regarded with extreme cynicism and hostility. There is no doubt that with sensitivity and an understanding of the emotions involved in this issue it is possible to overcome hostility and provide a very valuable service. Teachers working in this role can also be extremely useful in dispelling misconceptions amongst the staff in schools where they are based, and in providing them with practical help.

But the extent of such services is very limited at the moment and is likely to continue in this way. This means that the vast majority of West Indian children either have no contact or very little contact with help of this kind and spend the greatest part of their time with teachers who do not understand their problems and are sometimes unsympathetic towards them. The most realistic solution, therefore, would be to concentrate on the in-service training of all teachers working in multiracial schools rather than setting up additional 'supplementary' units.

The Community Relations Commission (CRC) and the Association of Teachers in Colleges and Departments of Education (ACTDE) (1974) point to the need for local authority appointments of advisors to co-ordinate this training and influence the direction of resources to multiracial education. They also recommend that experienced teachers in an area be drawn together to form a resource team whose functions might include providing courses and discussing the training needs of staff with head teachers. The educational needs of children in multiracial schools can only be met by a commitment on the part of the entire school. Solutions cannot be imposed by 'experts'. But if teachers are to be able to participate fully in policy making, they need access to information and resources and the time to consider and discuss appropriate strategies. These needs can only be met by in-service training.

It is also vitally important that all students leaving colleges and institutes of education should be adequately prepared for the multiracial classroom. At the moment this tends to be the domain of special-option courses, but a very persuasive argument can be put forward for it being an integral part of the training of every teacher. Even those students who have no intention of working in city schools may find ultimately that this is the only place where posts are available, since the number of vacancies in rural schools is far smaller than the demand for posts. In addition, the teaching profession is extremely mobile and even when a teacher starts work in a rural school, or a city school with few or no ethnic minority children, there is no guarantee that she will not work in an inner city school at some point in her career. Training all teachers for work in a multicultural society is therefore the only reasonable solution.

Innovatory approaches to language

Two main lessons can be learned from the American experience. First, attempts to curtail or denigrate the use of dialect are likely to be counterproductive, and to reinforce the subversive role of dialect in the school. All teachers are familiar with the use of Creole when children are in conflict situations: its unintelligibility is a weapon against the teacher and a symbol of group solidarity. Second, until more accepting attitudes are shown towards dialect and the culture and lifestyle of which it is a vital element, there is little hope that dialect speakers will be persuaded to use the standard language.

A number of innovatory approaches to language are discussed below in some detail. All are based on the assumption that the soundest approach to the teaching of standard English is to show that different dialects are accepted and appreciated by the school. For it is not until a child is a competent user of his own linguistic system that standard English will cease to be a threat.

Kaleidoscope: a school project

One very interesting experiment has been described by

Willsher *et al.* (1977). The George Salter High School, West Bromwich, began a five-year programme on language, class and culture (called 'Kaleidoscope') by trying to discover what the children thought of their own and each other's dialects. First-year pupils from 'middle ability' and 'slow learner' bands were played taped recordings of the various languages and dialects used by people in the school; these were identified and discussed. Afterwards children were presented with a questionnaire directed at the three main groups represented in the school: speakers of Black Country dialect, Indians and West Indians. Questions covered areas such as friends' reactions to their speaking standard English (would they be considered posh, playing the fool, or nice to listen to?); their ability to change the way they spoke; and the desirability of everyone speaking like television newsreaders.

The results of the questionnaire were worrying:

> The mother tongue/dialect of the vast majority of first year pupils seemed to be under attack from all sides, parental, peer, teacher and other elements of the local community, without any agency or institution whatsoever having realised or taken any positive initiatives to remedy the situation.

Teachers involved with the project were so disturbed by the negative views which children had of their speech, that they worked on a programme designed to 'rehabilitate' the various languages and dialects in the school. It was hoped that in so doing the children's self-esteem would be given a positive boost, as they came to realize that a range of language was both appreciated and accepted by the school. It was also felt that this would be a healthy starting point from which they might learn to operate effectively in standard English.

It is possible to approach this question in many different ways. Those involved in 'Kaleidoscope' at George Salter see their work as experimental, and teachers and pupils are continually learning from one another. They certainly do not claim to have found all the answers, but the details of the present programme may provide a useful starting point and basis for discussion for other schools and teachers whose interests lie in this direction.

Aim

This should attempt to ascertain attitudes towards own dialect/ language as a base line for later appraisal.

The programme

Could we sensitively and effectively do this?
Some suggestions:

(a) *Dialect*
What do teachers/pupils call the dialects:
Creole, patois, Brum, etc.
Do you speak Creole?
Do any of your family speak Creole?

Social perceptions:
Collect tapes of about ten different speakers (men and women) and make out an 'occupational' list, e.g.: teacher, dinner lady, carpenter, inspector, etc., and ask the children to match occupations to voices.

What do you think of the way the Queen speaks?

How do you react when you hear someone speaking Geordie or broad Yorkshire dialect?

Do you think there is a *best* English?
If so, who uses it?

Which of all the languages in the world would you most like to learn?
Why?

Have you ever heard of Esperanto?
It is a language made up of elements from English, French, Latin, German, etc., which is being developed as a universal language.
Why don't you think it has been taken up on a large scale?

(b) *Standard English*
Assess pupils' skills in using Standard English using own knowledge, referring back to notebooks etc.

113

Make a tape of a situation (e.g. an interview) in which someone uses dialect inappropriately.

Ask pupils to suggest (individually, in writing) where the responses could be improved.

Teaching

	Materials required
(a) *Language* *Survey* languages and dialects used by pupils/teachers/other staff in school	Tapes to be made Statistics: graph
Dialect and language Can you understand this? When does a dialect become a foreign language? Comparisons: pronunciation, vocabulary, grammar	Collect tapes of dialects represented in school, e.g.: Creolized English, 'Brum', 'West Bromwich', Indian English, other
The spoken v. the written language Transcribe tapes 'phonetically' Translate into standard English	Collect tapes of people, e.g. staff, in conversation, story, report
Appropriate register Who's speaking? Headmistress in Assembly, Minister, race commentator, comedian, etc. Who can you imitate?	Collect tapes: from school, radio, TV Tapes to be made

114

	Materials required
Languages in the school All languages equally efficient, easy/difficult, e.g. Eskimo Looking at school survey: ask individuals (parents?) to demonstrate their language (script, poetry, etc.) Language taught at school Which language would you most like to learn and why?	Some research

(b) *History*

Division of man's speech into languages: how did it happen?	Some research
History of written scripts	Books, other resources
Printing	

(c) *Science*

Animal communication	Film?
Man — speech — thought	
Speech reproduction	

(d) *Geography*
Local dialect map
Where the school's dialects and languages come from
Map of main world languages and approximate numbers using

(e) *Art*
Writing styles: materials and implements
Calligraphy (by-products: improved handwriting)

Materials required

Clay, 'papyrus', home-made paper, stylus, quills, etc.

Evaluation

Attempt to assess children's acceptance of their own and other people's dialects and their ability to 'switch' into standard English or their own dialect through a TV programme.

Programme may include:
News
Documentary
Interview
Situational comedy
Comedians
Sport
Reading or acting of Black Country 'Enoch and Eli' story

Written and spoken by children in appropriate style dialect

Production of *TV Times*

Timetable
Features
Advertisements
to demonstrate ability to, say, write about West Bromwich situation comedy in standard English.

Tell story in own dialect and then explain bits that can't be understood.

London Borough of Waltham Forest Supplementary Service for West Indian pupils

The programme suggested by teachers working on the Kaleidoscope project draws attention to the importance of giving

Creole and other non-standard varieties real status in the school. Acknowledging that a dialect is a valid linguistic system by discussing it openly in the context of language variation is a valuable first step, but other strategies must also be developed if the teacher is to create an atmosphere of true acceptance. Much of the pioneering work in this area has been done by the Waltham Forest Supplementary Service mentioned earlier in this chapter. This service provides resources for local teachers and employs peripatetic specialist staff who work in primary and middle schools in the area.

Unless the child feels free to use Creole, and unless his competence in Creole is fully acknowledged, he is likely to develop a sense of linguistic insecurity which may lead to him being labelled as 'inarticulate' or 'non-verbal'. Before the teacher can hope for fluency in standard English, the child must feel fully confident of the acceptability of the patterns he brings to the classroom, and this can be achieved in a number of ways. Teachers working with the Supplementary Service have found that various situations will quite spontaneously give rise to Creole, given an atmosphere of acceptance. Activities like card games and dominoes will often help younger children relax into Creole while certain discussion topics achieve the same effect in older children. These include relationships with other children; parental discipline; reporting an emotionally charged incident; food; smaller brothers and sisters; describing people; important happenings in the child's past.

Teachers have also found that playing taped stories is a very effective way of showing that all sorts of speech styles are valuable in their own right. This is an activity which is useful at all stages, but particularly with younger children. There are several sources for these recordings. Local radio will provide a variety of speakers, particularly in a cosmopolitan area. Various school broadcasts can also be useful. The Michael Rosen series 'That'd be Telling', for instance, was very well received. Organized around a particular theme, each programme included jokes, songs, stories and discussion presented by speakers with a wide range of different accents. And one component of the ILEA-sponsored 'Reading with Understanding' project, which we shall be looking at in great detail in the next chapter, is taped stories, again presented by actors from many different language backgrounds.

Oral work with the children can form the basis for stories, plays, dialogue and other written work, and can be particularly effective when tape recorders are used. The use of dialogue is of special interest since this is perhaps the most natural way of introducing Creole into writing. Stories and poems written in Creole are also helpful in encouraging the children to exploit their own language in writing.

Teacher initiatives

Teachers at George Salter High School and the Waltham Forest Supplementary Service have looked corporately at the language of the children they are working with, over the years, have developed various responses to the challenge of linguistic diversity. The Kaleidoscope project is of particular interest inasmuch as it affects an entire school. Teaching is across the curriculum and depends on an overall language policy of the kind which Bullock (1975) so strongly recommends. Of course, all pupils, and not only West Indian children, are likely to benefit from this approach. Although in many ways this represents an ideal situation, it should not detract from the fact that many teachers are regularly dealing with language matters with a great deal of imagination and sensitivity on an individual basis.

Natty Dread

One very persuasive example of teacher innovation which exploits many of the positive approaches already discussed is the work undertaken by Steve Hoyle at Santley Primary School, Brixton. He noticed that many of the children were interested in Natty Dread, a hero of reggae records, and thought it would be a good idea to use him for purposes of literacy. The first development was Natty Dread's ABC Book, an alphabet colouring book. Illustrations are multicultural and, in particular, West Indian. The words used reflect many different sources: records, the children themselves, Black teachers, popular cult figures and heroes.

M m

M is for
Muhammed Ali

mumma

mash up

magga

MARCUS GARVEY

mumma = mummy
mash up = destroy
magga = skinny

The colouring book produced very positive responses from Black and White children alike. They made a large colourful ABC collage which they hung around the school and this became something the children chanted as they moved about the building. The next development was a series of five stories which capitalized on Natty's appeal to the children. Titles included 'How Natty learned a lesson about Peace and Love' and 'How Natty led the children out of Babylon'. The text of the stories is largely standard English, but the dialogue is reported in Creole and the detail is distinctly West Indian. For instance, in 'How Natty led the children out of Babylon' (an adaptation of the 'Pied Piper of Hamlin'), Natty rids the city of rats by riding through the streets in an old lorry with his reggae band on the back.

> Natty and his band drove round the entire city and they completely emptied it of rats. They led the rats to the banks of the rivers of Babylon. Natty drove the truck out into the water with the music still playing. The rats followed the music until they drowned in the deep waters.
>
> 'By the rivers of Babylon ... where we sat down ...'

In triumph Natty and his band returned to the city and went to see the Prime Minister and his advisers,

> 'Hail, Minister!' Natty greeted the Prime Minister, 'Come farwud wid some dunny!'

But now that the rats had gone the Prime Minister and his cabinet changed their tune....

> 'Ah, yes! Jolly good! Well done Natty old chap! You seem to have done the trick. We're very proud of you ... now then ... about this money....'

The Prime Minister tried to explain to Natty how very short of money the country was. He couldn't really expect that he and his band deserved all that money, could he? Natty was very confused by all this and he listened to the Prime Minister with a stony face....

> 'Una did a mek a bargain wid we. I and I have rid dis town fe rats. Come farwud wid we dunny!'

Initially, the stories were read to the children; then they were produced in booklet form illustrated with drawings done by the children after they had heard the stories. The reactions from the children, West Indian and English alike, have been very enthusiastic. Natty is felt to be an important factor in getting children to read for pleasure and, because he is a very positive figure for the children to relate to, he often appears in their own work. There has also been a very encouraging response from some slow readers who have made enormous efforts to read through the materials. The reaction from the West Indian community, however, has been mixed. Although many younger Black teachers and community leaders have been in favour of the project, one parent group has expressed serious reservations. Parents' viewpoints obviously have to be respected but, hopefully, with fuller explanations of the aims of the work and what it is helping to achieve, they will be persuaded of its usefulness. In view of the popularity of Natty Dread and his apparent success in motivating children to both read and write, it would be a great shame if the idea were not allowed to develop further.

Dialect in practice

At the secondary level there is possibly greater scope for discussion of language and language difference and there is no doubt that many teachers are regularly handling the subject with considerable resourcefulness and sensitivity. Caroline Griffin's work in Tulse Hill School (reported in *Issues*, March, 1977) is an excellent example of how open discussion of dialect can lead to a greater understanding and appreciation of different language varieties.

Unsure of the attitudes of a third-year class towards dialect, she began with a story written in Somerset dialect called 'Summat Queer on Batch'. This was a dialect unfamiliar to everyone in the class and so represented no threat. After discussing the story and the strange vocabulary, one boy retold the story in his own words and then the class was asked to retell the opening in any dialect or accent they chose. This proved both interesting and entertaining and so the dialect theme was pursued with Cockney poems from the 'Billy the

Kid' collection. Boys were asked to copy out the poem they liked best and then rewrite it in standard English pointing out the differences between their version and the original and discussing the advantages of the dialect version.

One boy, a South African Asian, had written the poem in Jamaican Creole. The Jamaican dialect experts in the class were consulted and asked to correct it. By this time the whole class were very willing to experiment with dialect and accent and were obviously enjoying the material. They worked next in groups to put into their own words two dialect poems by Linton Kwezi Johnson, 'Double Skank' and the first part of 'Yout Scene', both of which deal with aspects of life in Brixton familiar to the boys. They were then asked to finish 'Yout Scene' in whichever dialect they chose. One West Indian boy, who had never previously used Creole in class, produced the following ending – in brackets – to the original poem.

Yout Scene

Last Satdey
I neva dey pan no faam
So I decide fetek a walk
doun a Brixton;
an see wha gwane.
de bredrin dem stan-up
outside a Hip City
as usual a look pretty;
dem a laaf lif laaf,
dem a talk dread talk,
dem a shuv and shuffle dem feet
soakin' in de sweet Musical Beat
but when nite come

(De Satdey scene change,
de recard shop lak
de pub dem jus de open,
de bad man dem jus de leave dem yard.
Brixton a bad place fe de a night time.
I forward de
And sight de yout dem wid some weed
A go fe ask dem fe a draw,
When I sight a knife,

122

An 'you money are yu life'
So I tun roun quick,
Kick the bwoy in a im seed,
Walk up a tek whe im weed,
Far I nar joke
When I sae Brixton is bad)

This work is not seen as an isolated project, but as part of an ongoing study of dialect difference. It has obviously proved stimulating and has led to a number of interesting developments. As Caroline Griffin points out, 'acknowledging the dialects which exist in the classroom within the broader context of dialect variation has made it less easy to put someone down by saying that what is different is also impossible to understand'.

Writing by young West Indians

Several teachers have capitalized on the literacy talents of their West Indian pupils and have produced collections of their work which is often of a very high quality. At the secondary level Geraldine McGuigan, working with children at Twyford Comprehensive School, Ealing, has edited a collection of prose, short stories, discussion and poems called 'Writing by young West Indians', much of which is in Creole. This work was done for the West Indian literature section of a Mode 3 English CSE syllabus, and was received enthusiastically by the children, some of whom had never written so much or at such length before. The collection was compiled partly as a stimulus for class discussion, and partly 'as a way of starting to document the experience of a new generation of West Indians who are beginning to write for themselves and for each other'. Meryl Philip, writing on the theme of Blackness, for example, has this to say:

De blackman

De blackman workin all night,
De blackman trousers fitting tight.
De blackman working eight day week,
de blackman na getting no sleep.

123

De blackman cleanin all you streets,
de Blackman can't even buy a sweets.
De Blackman doin all de cookin,
de whiteman standing der just lookin.
De blackman only wearing red,
de blackman gonna dead.

A very good example of work produced at a primary level which reflects a true acceptance of the multilingual and multicultural composition of the school, is the *Santley Lookout*, a magazine produced at Santley Primary School, Brixton, where Natty Dread first took to print. The children's work is reproduced as it is written and no attempt is made to 'correct' non-standard forms. And since there is a large West Indian population at the school, their writing often reflects their Creole background. Natty Dread, Annancy, Reggae, Rastafari and other West Indian themes are often to be found in the children's writing.

Rasta Man by Delroy of 2W

Rasta Man have wax hair.
Rasta Man wax him hair wid candles.
Rasta Man have long hair.
Rasta Man say Wa Da Da!
Rasta Man like long Beard
Rasta Man wear Red, Gold, Green and Black.
Red for the blood. Gold for the Sun.
Green for the Grass. Black for the tar.
Rasta Man say Rasta for I!

Children's jokes, songs and rhymes also feature prominently. June Watson of 2P, for instance, writes

You wan' a cigarette, sah?
No, sah!
Why, sah?
Because I gotta cold, sah!
Where d'you getta cold, sah?
Up de North Pole, sah!
What you doing dere, sah?
Catching Polar bear, sah!
How many did you get, sah?

One, sah!
Two, sah!
De rest got me, sah!

Any work along these lines is likely to enhance the child's confidence in the way he speaks and, consequently, his self-concept. The number of contributions by children and the sales figures for each issue certainly indicate that this is the case.

Language, literacy and other areas of the curriculum

Some of the examples discussed above have been undertaken by specialist English teachers in the secondary school; others have been considered primarily the domain of the English lesson in the primary school. However, language is central to almost all activities in the classroom, and other areas of the curriculum can also be used for reinforcing children's language skills.

Valerie Glass (1976), for instance, has suggested a particularly imaginative and successful procedure for primary school children's cookery lessons. She gets children to write down their recipes, listing ingredients and utensils. If the recipe is not too time consuming and the ingredients are not too expensive, and if the finished product can be shared out so that everybody in the class can have a taste, the child is allowed to buy the ingredients, and chooses three friends to cook with him.

The situation in which child becomes teacher is an interesting one: it allows him to practise skills of exposition which he seldom has a chance to use inside the classroom and his 'pupils' may be less inhibited in questioning him than their 'real' teacher. There is also ample opportunity for introducing new vocabulary and comparing words in different dialects and languages. An interesting development has been for children to repeat a recipe with an infant class, trying out their teaching skills in a new setting. Booklets containing the children's recipes have been duplicated and widely circulated, and the reactions of all concerned — parents, children, teachers and visitors — have been enthusiastic.

Steve Hoyle has found music a useful starting point for a wide range of language activities. For instance, in response to a song by Dennis Alcapone which contained the line

Me seh she come from Jamaica
And she daddy is a baker

the class composed a rhythmic chant along the following lines:

Me seh she come from Guyana
And she nyam off banana.

Me seh she come from Spain
Where it never never rain.

Me seh she come from de Congo
And she play on de Bongo.

The music teacher helped them to develop a tune using percussion instruments and later it was made into a dance, complete with costumes. The class of first-year juniors went on to perform at the Commonwealth Institute before an audience of more than a thousand. The children were obviously delighted with the experience. They wrote about the performance for the school magazine. They also copied silhouettes of all the countries featured in the song on to individual posters, which they decorated with the words of the song. In short, they had travelled a very long way in response to a familiar 'patois' phrase. The opportunities of using other aspects of the curriculum for language work, as these two brief examples serve to show, are unlimited.

A difference of degree

Many of the innovations considered in this chapter have been relevant to the teaching of children from a wide range of linguistic backgrounds, and not simply to the teaching of West Indians. It can be argued that the special position of West Indian children in our schools is a difference of degree rather than a difference of kind. When the Indian or Greek Cypriot child does not understand his British teacher, the teacher appreciates his difficulties and does not necessarily dismiss him as slow or stupid. Ironically, the working-class English child may be at a greater disadvantage in this respect, and the non-standard features in his speech may evoke the stereotype of the working-class child as inarticulate.

The West Indian is at a greater disadvantage still. In early encounters with the standard English of the teacher there may be comprehension difficulties which result in either an inappropriate response or not response at all. The teacher who does not appreciate this problem may find it all too easy to label the child as 'slow learning' or 'unintelligent', to an even greater extent than his working-class peers. There is evidence of a linguistic hierarchy where middle-class speech — and speakers — are given highest status, followed by working-class speech and, finally, West Indian speech.

It is the responsibility of the school to create an atmosphere of acceptance of all the children in its care and this involves an acceptance of their language. Ironically, appreciation of the child's dialect is the most likely route to the acquisition of standard English: building on linguistic competence leads to confidence; denigrating language leads to introversion and rejection. The linguistic and social stereotyping of West Indians is so widespread that very positive measures must be taken in all aspects of the curriculum to counteract the damage which has been done.

Chapter 7

Curriculum change for a multicultural society

The main focus of this book has been language. Where there are marked differences between the language of a particular group of children and that of the school, it is clearly the responsibility of teachers to inform themselves about the difficulties that this may pose for the children, and to consider the most effective ways of dealing with the situation. In many ways, however, this only represents a starting point. Language cannot be seen in isolation, and the focus of discussion must broaden at this point to include wider aspects of the curriculum.

There is a great deal of ambivalence about the kind of education which should be provided for children from different ethnic and cultural backgrounds. It has been established beyond doubt that West Indians and other ethnic minority members face widespread discrimination in housing, employment and the provision of services (Daniel, 1968; Smith, 1977). Many teachers recognize the importance of a strong sense of cultural identity in combating racism. Yet often they feel that it is not within the scope of the school to teach children about the history, religion and culture of their countries of origin. The Community Relations Commission (1977) reports various teacher comments to this effect:

> I honestly don't see it's the job of our schools to cater for other traditions and backgrounds for other people. I think if they come here they should accept the country and

conform to our standards and if they wish to keep their own culture around them they can do it privately.

I do honestly think we ought not to spend much time discussing the differences between them. We want them to take it all for granted and when they've been brought up in the infant schools side by side, they really don't think about coming from different social backgrounds.

Attitudes such as these have been the corner-stone of British schools' response to children from different cultures. They underestimate, however, the harmful effects of a curriculum based exclusively on Britain and British values. Milner's (1975) review of the research makes it quite clear that Black children are showing a strong preference for the dominant White group and a tendency to devalue their own group. This is a development which is likely to be damaging for immigrant and indigenous populations alike. As Stern and Wallis (1977) point out,

This devaluation of blackness has implications for the health of the individual, for the minority racial communities and for the general public. For the black British child, a desire to deny his colour is a denial of part of himself, highly detrimental to individual development and mental health. For the minority it leads to a lack of confidence in the potential of the group to contribute to society, and to an acceptance of inferior social and political status. For society as a whole, it represents a perpetuation of racialism and acts as an impediment to the achievement of racial equality.

The Race Relations Act (1976) recognizes these dangers and will have serious repercussions in the field of education. Although not intentionally discriminatory, many current practices put minority-group children at a disadvantage. Syllabuses based exclusively on a British cultural framework are more familiar to indigenous children than to immigrants. Libraries containing books which deal only with White characters and White values can also be interpreted as discriminatory. Nor are schools behaving in the best interests of their pupils when they fail to provide facilities for Punjabi or Gujarati children to study their mother tongue.

Local authorities are under an obligation to review their present policies and develop new ones. More attention will have to be given to minority languages and cultures, and greater help to community groups already involved in teaching language culture and religion. More emphasis will be required on the in-service training of teachers if they are to be equipped to work in multicultural schools. And libraries will have to spend their allowances on books which reflect the multiracial composition of present-day Britain. The major reappraisal of education required by the 1976 Act is also in line with an EEC directive that the mother tongue and culture of the countries of origin should be taught alongside other subjects.

ILEA have responded by setting up two projects designed to give greater support to teachers in multi-ethnic schools. The first – the Lambeth Whole School Project – involves a development team of six members who will work in a group of primary and secondary schools in central Lambeth. They are to concentrate on the development of school organization, curriculum and materials, and also school, parent and community relations. Their progress is to be monitored for dissemination through ILEA. The second project is a resources project. Curriculum resources drawn mainly from African, Caribbean and British Afro-Caribbean sources are to be collected, classified and organized into curriculum units which will be piloted in schools and monitored.

But the benefit of any such change of emphasis will be felt not only by ethnic minority children. Curriculum change is important for indigenous White children, too. Jeffcoate (1977) explains the importance of a multiracial curriculum for all children thus:

> The majority of my pupils are white; in multiracializing the English curriculum I most emphatically want to carry them with me. The changes I have made are as much for them as for black and Asian children ... because I want them to find the English classroom a more interesting and stimulating place to be.

Strategies for curriculum change

There is an urgent need for curriculum change. The precise

form which this change should take, however, is something about which most people are unclear. Many teachers have perceived the need for the school to reflect the multicultural composition of present-day Britain but have lacked the resources and overall strategies which are necessary for them to be effective. It is not enough, for instance, to devote one morning assembly to the celebration of Hindu Diwale, or a few weeks of geography to a project on the Caribbean, if the cultures of minority group children are given little or no recognition at other times.

It is also important that teachers should be aware of children's views on other cultures if they are to avoid reinforcing negative stereotypes. Jeffcoate *et al.* (1978), for instance, report that White children's ideas of ethnic minorities fit into two main categories: the image of the starving child and the image of the primitive native. Efforts of teachers using materials which reinforce these images without making reference to the validity of other cultures, and the range of individuals and life-styles within them, are likely to be counterproductive.

Clearly, we need to think very carefully about the kind of learning experiences which we offer children. One of the most helpful statements in this area has been formulated by Jeffcoate (1975) as part of his work on the Schools Council/ NFER 'Education for a multiracial society' project. He suggests the following criteria for the selection of learning experiences:

(a) An insular curriculum, preoccupied with Britain and British values, is unjustifiable in the final quarter of the twentieth century. The curriculum needs to be both international in its choice of content and global in its perspective.

(b) Contemporary British society contains a variety of social and ethnic groups; this variety should be made evident in visuals, stories and information offered to children.

(c) Pupils should have access to information about racial and cultural differences and similarities.

(d) People from British minority groups and from other cultures overseas should be represented as individuals with every variety of human quality and attribute. Stereotypes of minority groups in Britain and of cultures overseas, whether expressed in terms of human characteristics, life-styles, social roles or occupational status, are unacceptable and likely to be damaging.

(e) Other cultures and nations have their own validity and should be described in their own terms. Wherever possible, they should be allowed to speak for themselves and not be judged exclusively against British or European norms.

This approach is therefore all-embracing and covers not only the content of what is taught but also the 'hidden curriculum' which embodies the tacit beliefs and values of the school. It requires that the multiracial and multicultural composition of present-day Britain be acknowledged as an integral part of all school subjects and all school activities.

The things which surround the children in the classroom, for instance, can tell a great deal about a school's commitment to a multiracial society. The possibilities are limitless, particularly in the infant school: ready-mixed light and dark brown paint for art work; West Indian head ties, saris and Indian jewellery for dressing up; Asian cookery utensils, Black and Asian dolls, Afro combs and West Indian newspapers for the Wendy House. It is not suggested that these materials should replace the things normally found in home corners, simply that they are useful additions. They can be played with or ignored and no one need feel threatened by this essentially low-key approach. In fact, children tend to be very adaptive in this area: the Afro comb, for example, is generally regarded as another kind of comb by the other children. For ethnic-minority children, however, familiar objects of this kind represent a link between home and school and provide many valuable opportunities for discussion with the teacher.

Throughout the school the use of posters, tapes and other audio-visual aids is very important. Films, filmstrips, slides and cassettes particularly suitable for the multicultural classroom are available; so, too, are wall charts and other teaching materials. Various teacher guides and resource packs have been prepared and a list of agencies supplying these materials is included in Appendix B. There is also a list of magazines and sources of visuals for work cards.

If schools are to respond to the needs of all pupils, curriculum reform on a very large scale is required and the present discussion can only serve as the briefest of introductions. Given limitations of time and space, it is felt that the most useful approach is to concentrate on matters of general concern, and treatment of specific areas of the curriculum is restricted to suggestions for further reading (pp. 146-9). Many questions might be considered at this point and those chosen for special attention below in no way represent an exhaustive inventory of relevant issues. They are, however, areas of particular concern for many teachers and educators interested in reflecting the multicultural structure of present-day Britain.

Black Studies

The curriculum reform which is so urgently required entails such a complete revision of textbooks, syllabuses and teacher training that it can only realistically be envisaged as a long-term project. Many teachers and members of the West Indian community regard Black Studies as a viable interim measure, since the needs of West Indian children are too urgent to await the necessary changes in the curriculum. Black Studies represents a positive, if controversial, approach to the problems of poor self-concept. Pollack (1972a) explains the rationale behind such courses in this way:

> The purpose of a Black Studies Course is to provide both black and white peoples with a means of compensating for the inadequacies of understanding, lack of identity and poor self-image, sheer ignorance, the holding of myths and prejudices, feelings of superiority and hostility so that a degree of understanding may lead to mutual respect. This may be Utopian, but no more so than many syllabuses in various subjects.

Race relations, however, is a very sensitive area and, as a result, both the subject matter and the very idea of Black Studies have provoked considerable controversy.

The content of Black Studies courses can be analysed into two main components: a reinterpretation of history and an analysis of the contemporary situation. Although there is obviously variation between different courses, certain dominant

133

themes can be clearly distinguished. All syllabuses deal with Africa before the advent of the European in an attempt to counter the mythology of pre-colonial Africa as the 'Dark Continent'. Europe's need for economic expansion is discussed, as are the practice and ideology of the European slave trade, and its effects on the African population. Attention is paid to the agitation against slavery in Europe and in the Caribbean, and to Abolition and Emancipation and their repercussions on life in the Caribbean and USA. Finally, there is an examination of more recent history, including the development of Africa since the Berlin conference of 1885, Caribbean independence movements and the present situation, and Afro-American developments since Reconstruction.

One of the reservations which has been voiced against the historical aspect of Black Studies is that it may simply be replacing one biased account of history for another. Although by no means all accounts of Afro-American-British history are racist in nature, there is indisputably an imbalance of unbiased reporting and it can be argued that, at present, Black Studies may be seen as an attempt to redress this imbalance and to extend existing knowledge. As such, a case can be made for it being of value to both Black and White students whose common history it discusses.

The other component of Black Studies is the analysis of the contemporary situation. There is discussion of the present position in Africa and the Caribbean, though the main emphasis tends to be on the racial situation in the USA and Britain. In a British context, there is a concern for the position of immigrants, with special emphasis on problems in housing, employment and education. As well as considering the psychology of racism and prejudice, an outline is given of the practice and methodology of statutory race relations bodies, and to parliamentary legislation on race relations and immigration.

Inasmuch as Black Studies is concerned with drawing attention to the ills of present society and discussing how these ills might be eradicated, it can be seen to have political implications, although similar observations might be made about other subjects in the area of social studies. Many people fear the potentially divisive effects of this approach and feel therefore that it should be discouraged. Giles (1977), however, considers this argument to be misguided and suggests that the demand for Black Studies courses is rather a response to the divisive effects of racism and prejudice which already exist.

Only by making their response to racialism, and the social disadvantage based on colour prejudice, a legitimate concern of the schools curriculum, can the schools hope to bridge the widening gap in communication between the education system and black youth. Failure to give the needs and concerns of black students consideration through the schools will only lead to further alienation and isolation, the consequences of which will be the very separatism and division, based on race and colour, which many schools now deplore as detrimental to harmonious relations between all groups.

A case can certainly be made for extending present provisions for Black Studies courses. ILEA publish packs on Black Studies and aim to promote the subject as a key element within a broader, multicultural approach to the curriculum. There is also a demand for Black Studies courses outside the education system in the supplementary or Saturday schools which the West Indian community is organizing for its children. As an interim measure, while progress is being made towards total curriculum reform, there is little doubt that Black Studies can make an important contribution in promoting the self-respect and self-help motivation which are essential if young Blacks are to compete on equal terms in British society.

Books for a multiracial society

Books which reflect the multiracial composition of present-day Britain are obviously important. All too often, however, books which reflect a White world with White values dominate school bookshelves and libraries. The tendency to stereotype people from other cultures in fiction and non-fiction, and to omit the achievements of other civilizations from history and geography textbooks, has been discussed extensively elsewhere (Appendix C contains a list of critiques of racial bias and stereotyping in books). The importance of being alert to

135

practices of this kind must be stressed, but it is felt to be more helpful at this point to direct the reader to books which portray ethnic minorities in a positive light, and to restrict discussion in the main to materials which reflect contemporary Britain.

Although the number and quality of books which feature Black and Asian children is increasing all the time, they still make up only a very small proportion of all the books available. All the same, a small number of reading schemes, including popular ones like Sparks (Longman), Nippers (Macmillan) and Breakthrough (Longman), feature minority-group children in some of their stories. Sunstart (Ladybird) and the New West Indian Readers (Nelson), two schemes designed for the Caribbean but also marketed in Britain, reflect a multiracial society in which Black people are in the majority. Of course, the fact that a book or series is suitable for use in a multicultural setting does not necessarily mean that it is good in other respects. The New West Indian Readers, for instance, have a distinctly 'Janet and John' flavour:

> Here comes the big red van
> 'Come, Ann. Get me some jam from the van'.
> Sam and Ann ran to the van.
> The old man in the van sold Ann the jam.
> 'I have some jam. Do you want jam?'
> 'Oh yes, we want jam'.
> Sam and Ann took the jam and ran to the hut.

On a more positive note, however, there is a wide range of very acceptable picture story books set in England, America, the Caribbean, Africa and India. There is also a wealth of folk tales and myths from many different and varying backgrounds. A number of writers of children's fiction, incuding Nina Bawden and Farukh Dhondy, use Black and Asian characters in their books, and initiatives like the Collins competition for children's literature which reflects multiracial Britain are clearly to be welcomed. There is, of course no shortage of Black fiction from Caribbean, American and African writers.

English course books and anthologies often include multiracial illustrations and themes, though the extent varies considerably. There is also a number of very good reference and information books and some junior topic books which use multicultural material. Readers interested in finding out more about any of the categories mentioned above should consult one or more of the excellent bibliographies listed in Appendix C.

Reading Through Understanding

The materials produced by the 'Reading Through Understanding' project undertaken at the Centre for Urban Educational Studies deserve particular attention inasmuch as they offer a very positive view of multicultural Britain. The project was set up by the ILEA to investigate the teaching of reading in multi-ethnic schools, with particular reference to West Indian children. Attention has been paid not only to understanding the reading process, and the classroom as a context for learning to read, but also to understanding the impact of race and culture on the teaching/learning process. An interesting outcome of this approach has been that the materials they have produced are felt to be of value not simply for West Indian children, but for all children, whether in multicultural or all-White schools.

The materials consist of three complementary units. The first, 'Make-a-Story', is aimed at children in the five-to-eight age range and is a series of stories about a group of children living in a multiracial urban setting. The materials are aimed at encouraging reading to grow out of listening, and enabling children to build and read simple books based on enjoyable stories. In this sense the scheme is seen as supporting the early reading of all children, but it is of special value to urban children who can identify with recognizable and interesting facets of city life. It is also hoped that 'Make-a-Story' will develop the self-confidence of Black children and increase their enthusiasm for reading by providing stories and illustrations about children like themselves.

'Share-a-Story' is a collection of folk stories from Africa and the Caribbean aimed at children in the five-to-eleven age range and presented on cassette and in book form. The cassettes have been recorded by actors with appropriate accents, and are designed for use in a wide range of situations: by the teacher for story-telling; by individual children, either with cassette support or by themselves as their reading ability increases; and with groups of varying sizes, with the teacher's help or independently.

The third unit, 'Explore-a-Story', consists of a series of stories for children from nine to thirteen. There are two kinds of stories: folk tales, and true stories of people and events from all over the world. The folk tales are grouped into sets which explore a particular theme, such as mistaken identity or secret names. The true stories are about lesser-known men and women like Rani of Jhansi, a Joan of Arc figure from India, and Marcus Garvey, the Jamaican national hero. The aim is to develop an awareness of different cultures in all children and to enhance the self-concept of minority-group children.

Black British authors

West Indians have been described by Berry (1977) as 'grossly underexplored, underexpressed, underproduced and under-contributing'. There is, however, a small but very varied and stimulating range of work produced by Black British writers and, inasmuch as they reflect the Black experience in England rather than America or the Caribbean, this represents a very valuable development.

Relatively few collections of British West Indian writers have been published, though West Indian poetry, in both dialect and standard English, is often to be found in journals like *Limestone, Poetry Review* and *London Magazine*. The quality, range and variety of *Bluefoot Traveller: An Anthology of Westindian Poets in Britain* (1977) makes it clear, however, that the shortage of published materials cannot be attributed to a shortage of talent. Each of the contributors is highly individual, but a common thread runs through their writing — the experience of being Black in a White-dominated society. The strong oral tradition of the West Indies is to be seen in many of the poems. Frank John's poem, 'Me Soul', for instance, was clearly intended to be spoken rather than read, and was designed for a dramatic delivery:

Me soul on fire
A 'angin' on barbed wire
A wonder if to call de
Neighbour to put out
Me fire.
Ooooh noooo Ooooh no
Oh oh oh oh
How me heart beatin' so
Oh oh oh oh
Oh Gawd oh
How long A could stand
This hunger blow
Oh oh oh oh
Oh yes
It leavin' me poor flesh
In distress
Oh oh oh oh
Oh oh yes yes
Me body can't resist
Dis violen unrest
No no oh oh
Oh oh
Me soul talkin'
Me soul walkin'
Me soul talkin' to me
Boop boop boop boop
Break loose.

Linton Kwesi Johnson, an accomplished and highly polished young writer who contributes to *Bluefoot Traveller*, has published two collections of his work: 'Voices of the Living and the Dead' and *Dread Beat and Blood* Johnson is another in the tradition of 'oral poets' and his powerful delivery can be heard in 'All We Doin is Defendin/Five Nights of Bleedin' (Virgin Records Vs 19012), two of his poems set to reggae music. His subject matter is firmly based in the West Indian community and many teachers who have used his work have been struck by the immediate response it has produced in young Black pupils. He describes his style as a result of the tension which exists between Jamaican English and Jamaican Creole and between those and British English. The result is impressive:

Same way
deep to the depth of anguish
is where
the search must dive, aflame
right down to where ...
the sound is like the echo of the belly of the ground;
deep doun low where the anger grows, harshly.

blazin the voice has to be,
like lightning,
lighting up the sky so moon,
rakin' up the dark place,
showing up the foe an the way he makes his moves low,
loud in its tone of thunder, hot.

the way cannot be but blood
the song
of mud caught up in the blood, dying,
holdin' on to life
but dying all the same, yet livin out the pain.
the end cannot be but sweet, final.

Several writers, notably Samuel Selvon, Andrew Salkey
and V. S. Naipaul, who were born in the West Indies but are
now resident in England, have written short stories and novels
which deal with the British situation. There is a strong feeling
of a West Indian identity in the work of these writers. In the
Caribbean the differences between islands strung in an archi-
pelago almost two thousand miles long makes the idea of a
collective identity politically unviable. The British failure to
perceive these differences, however, has tended to draw the
various islanders together. As Salkey (1969) explains, 'The
blanket term West Indian doesn't exist in the West Indies; it
does in London, has to for protection's sake.'

Social issues, and particularly housing, not surprisingly pre-
occupy these writers. Selvon's work (*Ways of Sunlight; I Hear
Thunder; The Housing Lark; The Lonely Londoners*) draws
heavily on working-class heroes whose problems arise partly
from their race, partly from their class. The characters of
Naipaul (in *A House for Mr Biswas*; *A Flag for the Island*) and
Salkey (in *The Adventures of Catullus Kelly*), however, tend
to be middle class and educated and, as such, are protected

from at least some of the indignities which Selvon's characters experience.

Dialect plays an important part in many of these works. Naipaul and Salkey reserve Creole for dialogue, as does Selvon in his earlier work. However, 'Down in the Main', a short story from *Ways of Sunlight*, is written wholly in dialect; and *The Lonely Londoners* also makes extensive use of dialect.

In addition to these established writers and poets, there is an increasing number of publications featuring the work of young West Indians still at school. Paul George, a Grenadian now living in Southall, wrote *Memories* when he was sixteen. The first part, as the title suggests, is an account of childhood experiences in the West Indies; the second part consists of poems on the theme of Blackness. *In the Melting Pot* was written by another young author, Chelsea Herbert, while still a student at a college of further education. Essentially a love story, it provides an interesting perspective on West Indian family life and some aspects of youth culture. *Stepping Out* is an anthology of verse, prose and short plays written by nine 15-year-old West Indians when still at school. (It contains much of the work first produced as 'Writing by Young West Indians' which is mentioned in the discussion of teacher initiatives in Chapter 6.) *Stepping Out* is divided into seven different sections (titles include 'Why don't West Indian talk West Indian?', 'Prejudice: What is it?' and 'New in age, but not in rage'), each of which discusses areas of vital concern to young Blacks.

Jennifer Johnson, a young British-born Black of Jamaican parentage, has had two short studies ('Ballad for you' and 'Park Bench Blues') published in *Race Today*, January 1978. The stories were produced at a creative writing and drama workshop set up at a Brixton Youth Centre. They are highly polished and entertaining. Jennifer Johnson writes exclusively in Creole and deals with the experiences of young Black people in Britain, seen particularly from a Black girl's perspective. She is a natural story-teller and her attention to detail and lively dialogue are impressive.

The youngest West Indian writer to appear in print is Accabre Huntley. *At School Today* is a collection of poems written when she was nine years old. They are remarkable for their perception of the problems which beset Black people in

141

a White majority. But her writing is essentially confident and optimistic and there is an unmistakable sense of pride in herself and in her people:

I am black
as I thought
My lids are brown
as I thought
My hair is curled
As I thought
I am free
as I know!

Ethnic-minority adults

It can hardly escape the attention of ethnic-minority children that the adults from their communities usually occupy low-status positions in society. This is particularly acute in the case of West Indian children. Black lawyers, Black doctors and Black executives are rare; Black workers in public transport, factories and hospitals are plentiful. Interest in Black studies has uncovered a whole range of historical figures for children to emulate, but it is equally important that they should see present-day minority-group adults in high-status positions in society and there are several ways in which the school can help.

Parents are a very valuable resource. A project which involved looking at various aspects of work could easily draw on the expertise of ethnic-minority adults. Similarly, a project on school which examined the experiences of people in different places or at different times could be brought to life by outside speakers, including parents of minority-group children. Cookery lessons provide another opportunity for involving parents.

The growing number of West Indian poets, authors and actors is another useful source of high-status Black adults. Writers like Samuel Selvon and Linton Kwesi Johnson give regular readings of their work to school children and are very enthusiastically received. Black theatre and dance groups, although in short supply, have also been used very successfully.

142

But perhaps the most valuable local resource is the Black musician. Many schools treat their Steel Band as an after-school activity organized by a teacher with a particular interest in music, but an increasing number of local authorities are appointing West Indian tutors to teach the children during school time. This is an important step forward in according the Steel Band the same status as other subjects on the curriculum rather than something simply for pleasure.

The potential of the Steel Band is enormous. As well as developing the musical skills of the children, it is possible to link the Band with other aspects of their work. Liaison between Band tutors and classroom teachers, for instance, can lead to work on its Caribbean heritage. There is no shortage of source material in the form of records, and photographs, and also parents who can talk to the children from their first-hand experience.

But just as important is the status which school and players derive from the Band. Several Bands have gone beyond performances in school assemblies and concerts to make records and play for local radio or even television. West Indian children are always well represented in the Bands, and even those who do not take part have the satisfaction of seeing an especially West Indian activity receiving recognition in the school. As one teacher in a school which had recently introduced a Steel Band observed, it has provided 'the chief means of giving status to West Indians where none was previously accorded'.

A difference of degree again

It was proposed in Chapter 6 that West Indian language differences were differences of degree rather than differences of kind. We find a similar situation when we come to consider cultural differences. It is generally recognized that Chinese, Indians, Pakistanis, Greeks and Turks have an ancient and eminently respectable cultural heritage, not least by the children from these cultures themselves. Again, working-class British children may be at a greater disadvantage in this respect: there is a widespread feeling that working-class and poorer families, regardless of race or colour, are 'culturally deprived' and it is only as a result of enterprises like Rosen's 'Language and Class Workshop' and 'Centerprise' publications that the wealth of working-class culture has begun to make an impact. Black culture, however, is generally assigned status even lower than working-class culture. The impression of the Black as savage, stupid and indolent has been part of the English caricature for so long that little evidence has ever been given to the intrinsic value of Black culture. It is important that the culture of all children should be recognized and accepted by the school. But it is particularly important in the case of Black children, if we are seriously concerned that the present patterns of underperformance should be reversed.

There is a large and very respectable body of research (reviewed by Milner, 1975) which points to the fact that small children are extremely sensitive to racial difference. White children show in-group preferences, Black and Asian children show preferences for the dominant White society. White children's stereotypes of ethnic minorities are also a cause for concern (Jeffcoate *et al.*, 1978). There is an equally large and respectable body of research which demonstrates that ethnic minorities face widespread discrimination in employment, housing and the provision of services (Daniel, 1968; Smith, 1977). The findings in both areas point to an urgent need for curriculum change.

The implementation of such change is likely, however, to meet with considerable resistance from all sections of society, not least from teachers. There seems to be an unswerving faith in the fairmindedness of the British people. There is a similar confidence that young children do not perceive racial differences, nor do they make judgments on the basis of race. When presented with very strong evidence to the contrary, the reaction is very often one of disbelief and anger. An interesting example is the controversy over the report of Schools' Council/NFER 'Education for a Multiracial Society' project. According to various press sources, the report was dismissed by representatives of the NUT as a poorly researched document which read like a political treatise. There was a general feeling that the authors of the report were unduly critical of teachers, but as the *New Society* editorial of 9 February 1978 points out:

The NUT is not helping its members by blocking the publication of a report which shows that teachers' work on race relations is in a very difficult context. Truth is often awkward. But there's no future in trying to hide it.

All the indications are that we are not meeting the legitimate needs of children from ethnic minorities, and that the consequences of our unwillingness to change will be extremely harmful both for them and for indigenous White children. Yet multiculturalism in education is an exciting challenge. Many schools and teachers are already responding to this challenge by developing new and interesting approaches to the curriculum. In many ways this only represents a beginning, but it is none the less an important beginning.

Suggestions for further reading

Chapter 1 West Indians in Britain

For a good general introduction to all aspects of life in the West Indies, see *West Indian Societies* by David Lowenthal (Oxford University Press, 1972). The fullest discussion of West Indian immigration is to be found in Ceri Peach's *West Indian Migration to Britain: a Social Geography* (Oxford University Press, 1968) and E. J. B. Rose *et al.*'s *Colour and Citizenship: A Report on British Race Relations* (Oxford University Press/Institute of Race Relations, 1969). More recent statistics are contained in the *Select Committee's Report on the West Indian Community* (HMSO, 1977).

General discussion of the education of ethnic-minority children is contained in Joti Bhatnagar's *Immigrants at School* (Cornmarket Press, 1970); Gordon Bowker's *Education of Coloured Immigrants* (Longman, 1968); J. McNeal and M. Roger's *Multiracial School* (Penguin, 1971); and, more recently, in David Hill's *Teaching in Multiracial Schools* (Methuen, 1976) and Maurice Hobb's *Teaching in a Multi-Racial Society* (Association of Christian Teachers, 1976). Bernard Coard's *How the West Indian Child is made Educationally Sub-Normal in the British School System* (New Beacon Books, 1971) and Viv Edwards's *West Indian Language, Attitudes and the School* (National Association for Multiracial Education, 1977) deal specifically with West Indian children. Judith Haynes's *Educational Assessment of Immigrant Pupils* (National Foundation for Educational Research (NFER), 1971) is a useful review of the ways in which ethnic-minority children were assessed on arrival in Britain.

Discussions of the ways in which West Indians have adapted to life in Britain, other than those mentioned in the text, include Juliet Cheetham's *Social Work with Immigrants* (Routledge & Kegan Paul, 1972); Kathryn Fitzherbert's *West Indian Children in Britain* (Bell, 1976); the Lozell's

146

Social Development Centre's *Wednesday's Child. A report on under fives provision in Handsworth* (Community Relations Commission, 1975); and Delroy Louden's unpublished Ph.D. thesis (University of Bristol, 1977) 'The Comparative Study of Self-Concept, Self-Esteem and Locus of Control in Minority Group Adolescents in English Multiracial Schools'.

The growing alienation of Black youths from British society is documented in Derek Humphrey's *Police Power and Black People* (Panther, 1972). Rastafarianism is the subject of a book by L. E. Barrett (*The Rastafarians*, Heinemann, 1978) and its development in Britain is discussed in several articles by Barry Troyna, and, in particular, in *Rastafarianism, Reggae and Racism* (National Association for Multiracial Education, 1978).

Chapter 2 West Indian Creole

The focus of the description in Chapter 2 is the main areas of difference between Creole and standard English, and a complete description is well beyond the scope of this book. Readers who wish to find out more about Creole may wish to refer to the more technical descriptions available. These include B. L. Bailey's *A Transformational Grammar of Jamaican Creole* (Cambridge University Press, 1966); D. Bickerton's *The Dynamics of a Creole System* (Cambridge University Press, 1975) and J. Well's *Jamaican Pronunciation in London* (Blackwell, 1973). *A Dictionary of Jamaican English* by F. G. Cassidy and R. B. Le Page and a description dealing mainly with the vocabulary of *Jamaica Talk* by F. G. Cassidy (Cambridge University Press) are also available. The description of linguistic diversity in Jamaica over the centuries (p. 19) comes from *Creole Language Studies*, vol. II, edited by R. B. Le Page (Macmillan, 1961). Both vol. I (Macmillan, 1960) and vol. II contain interesting discussions of language in the West Indies.

Loretto Todd has written a general account of *Pidgins and Creoles* (Routledge & Kegan Paul, 1974). More technical aspects of this subject are dealt with in a collection of papers called *Pidginization and Creolization*, edited by Dell Hymes (Cambridge University Press, 1971), some of which discuss the situation in the West Indies.

Very little has been written on West Indian language use in Britain. The survey at the Midlands Comprehensive School mentioned on page 37 was undertaken with the help of Shirley Hadi, a member of the Schools Council/National Foundation for Educational Research (NFER) Multiracial Society project team. It is reported in 'A Multiracial High School Speaks' by Shirley Willsher *et al., Multiracial School*, Spring, 1977. David Sutcliffe is currently working on a book about the language of West Indians in Britain (Blackwell, forthcoming).

Chapter 3 Verbal skills in West Indians

Interesting treatments of standard and non-standard English are contained in Randolph Quirk's *The Use of English* (Longman, 1962), David Stringer's *Language Variation and English* (Open University Press, 1973) and Peter Trudgill's *Sociolinguistics* (Penguin, 1974). An account of theories of verbal deprivation is to be found in *Deprivation and Disadvantage?* by M. H. Moss (Open University Press, 1973). Two other Open University publications, *Language and Social Class: An Introduction to Bernstein's Sociolinguistics*, by D. Mackinnon (1977) and *Social Relationships and Language: Some Aspects of the Work of Basil Bernstein* by Victor Lee (1975), deal with the work of Basil Bernstein. The best source of Bernstein's own writings is *Class, Codes and Control* (Routledge & Kegan Paul, 1971).

Afro-American Anthology edited by N. Whitten and J. Szwed (Free Press, 1970) is a very useful collection of papers dealing with the language and culture of American and Caribbean Blacks. L. E. Barnett's *The Sun and the Drum: African Roots in Jamaican Folk Tradition* (Heinemann, 1977) is another interesting contribution to this area.

Chapter 4 Creole interference

A useful introduction to more recent theories of reading is contained in Frank Smith's *Understanding Reading: A Psycholinguistic Analysis of Reading and Learning to Read* (Holt, Rinehart & Winston, 1971). Again Open University publications provide highly readable accounts of developments in this field, notably *Reading Purposes, Comprehension and the Use of Context*, by N. C. Farnes (Open University Press, 1972).

Useful accounts of non-standard language and education are contained in *Teaching Black Children to Read* edited by J. Baratz and B. Shuy (Center for Applied Linguistics, 1969); *Teaching Standard English in the Inner City* (Center for Applied Linguistics, 1969); *Child Language and Education* by Courtnay Cazden (Holt, Rinehart & Winston, 1972) and *Accent, Dialect and the School* by Peter Trudgill (Edward Arnold, 1975).

Chapter 5 Language attitudes and educational success

The relationship between language and identity is very well documented. Some readable accounts are included in *Language and Poverty: Perspectives on a Theme*, edited by Frederick Williams (Institute for Research on Poverty, 1970) and David Stringer's *Language Variation and English* (Open University Press, 1973). Interesting discussions of this general area are also contained in *Language Attitudes: Current Trends and Prospects*, edited by R. Shuy and R. Fasold (Center for Applied Linguistics, 1973).

Chapter 6 Practical approaches to language

Geraldine McGuigan writes at greater length in *Multiracial School* (Summer 1976) on 'Talking and Writing by Black Fifth Formers'. Shirley Willsher and other members of the George Salter High School have described various aspects of school life in 'A Multiracial High School Speaks' in *Multiracial School*, Spring 1977. And Steve Hoyle has written an account of 'Street Language in an Urban Primary School' in *Issues in Race and Education* no. 12, January, 1978.

Suggestions for initial and in-service teacher training are contained in *Teacher Education for a Multicultural Society*, a joint report prepared by the CRC and ACTDE (1974), and in the CRE's *Urban Deprivation, Racial Inequality and Social Policy: A Report* (HMSO, 1977).

Chapter 7 Curriculum change for a multicultural society

Relatively little material has been published on developing aspects of the multiracial curriculum. Quite a lot of attention, however, has been paid to religion, and a notable contribution has been Schools Council Working Paper 36 *Religious Education in Secondary Schools* (Evans/ Methuen Educational, 1971). David Hill's *Teaching in Multiracial Schools* (Methuen, 1976) includes a discussion on Religious Education which draws on two Christian Education Movement publications: Owen Cole's *World Religions in Primary Schools* and Donald Butler's *World Religions in Secondary Schools*. The City of Birmingham's *Agreed Syllabus on Religious Education* (1975) is a useful source of ideas and materials suitable for a multicultural setting. The CRC publication, *World Religions: Aids for Teachers* (1972), is also very useful.

Some interesting discussion in the area of Social Studies is contained in Margaret Nandy's 'Social Studies for a Multiracial Society' (in J. Mc-Neal and M. Rogers (eds), *Multiracial School*), and Ann Dummett's 'A Walking Dead Man' (in the journal *Multiracial School*, Summer 1972). Two very stimulating and helpful articles on history, 'Cultural Relevance: Jamaican History and London Children' by Bev Woodroffe (*Issues in Race and Education*, November 1976) and 'History for a Changing World: Designing and Implementing a New Syllabus at Tulse Hill School' by Deirdre Sadgrove and Steve Smith (*Issues in Race and Education*, October 1977), contain specific suggestions for curriculum change.

Home Economics is the subject of an article by Yvonne Collymore which is reprinted in Hill (1976). Her suggestions are aimed mainly at secondary school teachers, but Valerie Glass has described some interesting ideas for cookery lessons with younger children. These have already been touched upon in Chapter 6, but are reported at length in *Teacher's World* 2 July 1976. Two CRC publications, *Afro Hair, Skin Care and Recipes* (1976), and *Caribbean Cookery* (1973), are also helpful.

More general suggestions for introducing elements of other cultures into the curriculum are contained in *Wider Horizons*, a teachers' handbook produced by the Bradford Directorate of Education. Mary Worrall's article, 'Curriculum Strategies for Multiracial Education' in *Multiracial School*, Summer, 1976 is also extremely helpful in terms of ideas and teaching materials for teaching children in the 5–13 range.

By far the most comprehensive work undertaken in this area is Rob Jeffcoate, Elaine Brittan, Shirley Hadi and Mary Worrall's *Multiracial Education: Curriculum and Context 5–13* (Schools Council 1977, unpublished). At the time of writing there is considerable controversy over the form in which it should be published (see *Times Educational Supplement*, 17 December 1977). Representatives of the National Union of Teachers (NUT) dislike the first part of the report which they feel is unduly critical of teachers and politically biased. The authors, on the other hand, consider that the first part provides the rationale for the curriculum suggestions which follow and hold that the report should be published as it stands. The publication of the proposed first chapter in *New Society* 17 February 1978 has, however, allowed readers to decide for themselves whether or not the criticisms are deserved. Hopefully, these problems will be resolved, as the report of the Schools Council project provides the most extensive and stimulating discussion to date of the subject of curriculum change.

Appendix A

Useful publications and where to get them

Journals and bulletins

New Equals. Bimonthly bulletin, available free of charge from the Commission for Racial Equality, Elliot House, 10/12 Allington Street, London SW1E 5EH.

Education Journal. Bimonthly education bulletin, available free from the CRE.

New Community. Quarterly journal of the CRE.

New Approaches to Multiracial Education. Journal of the National Association for Multiracial Education, published three times a year.

Two local NAME branches also publish bulletins:

Change is available from Valerie Glass, Shenton Primary School, Dunlin Road, Leicester.

Issues in Race and Education is available from 58 Collingbourne Road, London W12.

Race. Quarterly journal of the Institute of Race Relations, 249/279 Pentonville Road, London N1.

Race Today. Fortnightly journal, published by the Race Today Collective, 74 Shakespeare Road, London SE24 0PT.

Specialist bookshops and publishers

The following bookshops specialize in books from Africa and the Caribbean, and books which reflect the Black experience in Britain:

Bogle l'Ouverture,
5a Chignell Place,
London W13

New Beacon Books,
26 Stroud Green Road,
London N4 3EN

Harriet Tubman Books,
27/29 Grove Lane,
Handsworth,
Birmingham 21

The English Centre,
Ebury Teachers' Centre,
Sutherland Street,
London SW1

The English Centre is not a commercial organization but it supplies some materials to schools outside the ILEA, including *Memories* by Paul George and *The Melting Pot* by Chelsea Herbert in book and cassette form.

The Commonplace Workshop,
28 Dorset Road,
Ealing,
London W5
The Commonplace Workshop is a non-profit-making, self-help project whose aim is to encourage and support creative expression through the writing and arts of the community and to recognize, promote and publish this work.

Centerprise,
136/138 Kingsland High Street,
London E8
Centerprise is a bookshop based in a community centre in East London. As well as promoting various community activities, Centerprise has its own publishing project and has encouraged some very interesting work, including autobiographies of local working-class people.

Appendix B

Teaching materials for the multiracial classroom

Commission for Racial Equality,
Elliot House,
10/12 Allington Street,
London SW1E 5EH
In addition to the various bulletins and journals listed in Appendix A, the Commission for Racial Equality (CRE) supplies free of charge reprints from *Education and Community Relations* bound together in a teachers' information pack. Issues include teaching about race relations, Africa and the Caribbean. The CRE also produce a wide range of publications on matters of concern to ethnic minorities in Britain. Book exhibitions are available on loan and films can be hired.

ILEA Learning Materials Service,
Highbury Station Road,
Islington,
London N1 1SB
The Inner London Education Authority (ILEA) provides background material for teachers on children's countries of origin and multi-media packs on a variety of subjects including Black Studies and World History Themes. Some of these materials are available outside ILEA. Full details may be obtained on request.

Commonwealth Institute,
Kensington High Street,
London W8 6NQ
The Commonwealth Institute has a wide range of materials not only on the Commonwealth but on race relations and education in multicultural schools. The Education Department publishes teachers' guides, fact sheets and kits. The Library and Resources Centre lends books and audiovisual materials. The Shop sells various publications, audiovisual materials and craftwork.

Magazines (for work cards, etc.)

Orbit (a Zambian children's comic) from OXFAM Education Department, 274 Banbury Road, Oxford OX1 7D2 or VCOAD, 69 Victoria Street, London SW1.

Ebony (a Black American magazine) from bookstalls in Black areas.

African Women from New Beacon Books (address in Appendix A).

Africa from New Beacon Books (address in Appendix A).

New Internationalist (a magazine on development studies) from 62a High Street, Wallingford, Oxon.

Appendix C

Useful bibliographies

Critiques of racial bias and stereotyping

Children's Rights Workshop (eds), *Racist and Sexist Images in Children's Books*, available from Writers and Readers Publishers Cooperative, 233a Kentish Town Road, London NW5.

Dixon, R. (1977), *Catching Them Young: Sexist, Racist and Class Images in Children's Books*, Pluto Press.

Elkin, Judith (ed.) (1976), *Books for the Multiracial Classroom*, The Library Association.

Hill, J. (ed.) (1976), *Books for Children: The Homelands of Immigrants in Britain*, Institute of Race Relations.

Larrick, N. (1972), 'The All-White World of Children's Books' in D. MacCann and G. Woodward (eds), *The Black American in Books for Children*, Scarecrow Press, p. 160.

Liverpool Community Relations Commission (1974), *Sowing the Dragons Teeth – The Racial Bias in the Books We Teach*.

Proctor, C. (1975), *Racist Textbooks*, National Union of Students (NUS).

Books and audio-visual aids for multicultural education

Commission for Racial Equality, *A Bibliography for Teachers, Books for Under Fives in Multiracial Britain, A Guide to Audiovisual Aids, Public Library Service for a Multicultural Society*.

Day, Alison, *The Library in the Multi-Racial Secondary School: A Caribbean Book List* (available from the CRE).

Library Association Youth Libraries Group, Pamphlet no. 17, Books for the Multiracial Classroom.

New Beacon Books, Special Caribbean Book List for Teachers, Parents and Teenagers.

The Runnymede Trust, Ethnic Minorities in Britain. A Select Bibliography.

155

Bibliography

ABRAHAMS, R. D. (1970), 'Patterns of Performance in the British West Indies', in N. Whitten and J. Szwed (eds), *Afro American Anthology: Contemporary Perspectives*, New York, Free Press, pp. 163-78.

ABRAHAMS, R. D. (1972), 'The Training of the Man of Words in Talking Sweet', *Language in Society*, vol. 1, no. 1, pp. 15-30.

ALLEYNE. M. (1971), 'The Cultural Matrix of Creolization' in Hymes, 1971, pp. 169-86.

Association of Teachers of English to Pupils from Overseas (ATEPO) (Birmingham Branch) (1970), *Work Group on West Indian Pupils Report.*

BAGLEY, C. (1975), 'The Background of Deviance in Black Children in London', in Verma and Bagley, 1975, pp. 283-93.

BAGLEY, C. and COARD, B. (1975), 'Cultural Knowledge and Rejection of Ethnic Identity in West Indian Children in London', in Verma and Bagley, 1975, pp. 322-31.

BAGLEY, C. and VERMA, G. K. (1975), 'Inter-Ethnic Attitudes and Behaviour in British Multi-Racial Schools', in Verma and Bagley, 1975, pp. 236-62.

BAILEY, B. L. (1966), *A Transformational Grammar of Jamaican Creole*, Cambridge University Press.

BARATZ, J. (1969a), 'Teaching Reading in an Urban Negro School System', in Baratz and Shuy, 1969, pp. 92-116.

BARATZ, J. (1969b), 'Linguistic and Cultural Factors in Teaching Reading to Ghetto Children', *Elementary English*, vol. 46, pp. 199-203.

BARATZ. J. C. and SHUY, R. W. (eds) (1969), *Teaching Black Children to Read*, Washington D.C., Center for Applied Linguistics.

BENNETT, L. (1966), *Jamaica Labrish*, Jamaica, Songster's Book Stores.

BENNETT, L. (1966), 'Me and Annancy', in Jekyll, 1966, pp. ix–xi.

BEREITER, C. *et al.* (1966), 'An Academically Orientated Pre-School for Culturally Deprived Children', in F. M. Hechinger (ed.), *Pre-School Education Today*, New York: Doubleday, pp. 105–37.

BERNSTEIN, B. (1973), *Class, Codes and Control*, London, Routledge & Kegan Paul.

BERRY, J. (ed.) (1977), *Bluefoot Traveller: An Anthology of West Indian Poets in Britain*, Limestone Publications.

BICKERTON, D. (1975), *The Dynamics of a Creole System*, Cambridge University Press.

BLAIR, C. (1971), 'Immigrant Education and Social Class', *Race Today*, August.

BULLOCK, Sir A. (1975), *A Language for Life*, London, HMSO.

BURSTALL, C. (1968), *French from Eight: A National Experiment*, Windsor, National Foundation for Educational Research.

CARRINGTON, D. and BORELY (eds) (1977), *The Language Arts Syllabus, 1975: Comment and Countercomment*, University of Saint Augustine, Trinidad.

CASSIDY, F. G. (1971), *Jamaica Talk*, 2nd edn, London, Macmillan.

CASSIDY, F. G. and LE PAGE, R. B. (1967), *Dictionary of Jamaican English*, Cambridge University Press.

COARD, B. (1971), *How the West Indian Child is made Educationally Sub-Normal in the British School System*, London, New Beacon Books.

COMMUNITY RELATIONS COMMISSION (1974a), *Educational Needs of Children from Minority Groups*, London, Community Relations Commission.

COMMUNITY RELATIONS COMMISSION (1974b), *Unemployment and Homelessness: A Report*, London, Community Relations Commission.

COMMUNITY RELATIONS COMMISSION (1974c), *In-Service Teacher Training in Multi-Racial Areas – A Seminar Report*, London, Community Relations Commission.

COMMUNITY RELATIONS COMMISSION (1975), *Who Minds? A Study of Working Mothers and Childminding in Ethnic Minority Communities*, London, Community Relations Commission.

COMMUNITY RELATIONS COMMISSION (1977), *Urban Deprivation, Racial Inequality and Social Policy*, London, HMSO.

COMMUNITY RELATIONS COMMISSION and A.T.C.D.E. (1974), *Teacher Education for a Multi-Cultural Society*, London, Community Relations Commission.

CRYSTAL, D. (1976), *Child Language, Learning and Linguistics*, London, Edward Arnold.

DANIEL, W. W. (1968), *Racial Discrimination in England*, Harmonds-worth, Penguin.

EDWARDS, V. K. (1975), 'Can Dialect Cause Comprehension Problems for West Indian Children?', *Multiracial School*, vol. 4, no. 2.

EDWARDS, V. K. (1976), *West Indian Language, Attitudes and the School*, London, National Association for Multiracial Education.

EDWARDS, V. K. (1978a), 'Language Attitudes and Underperformance in West Indian Children', *Educational Review*, vol. 30, no. 1.

EDWARDS, V. K. (1978b), 'Dialect Interference in West Indian Children', *Language and Speech*, vol. 21, part 1.

EDWARDS, V. K. and SUTCLIFFE, D. (1977), 'When Creole can be King', *Times Educational Supplement*, 18 March.

FAGAN, S. F. U. (1958), 'Analysis of the Written Language English of Some Jamaican City Children', Unpublished M.A. thesis, University of London.

FARB, P. (1973), *Word Play*, London, Jonathan Cape.

FIELD, F. and HAIKIN, P. (1971), *Black Britons*, Oxford University Press.

FRENDER, R., BROWN, B. and LAMBERT, W. E. (1970), 'The Role of Speech Characteristics in Scholastic Success', *Canadian Journal of Behavioral Science*, vol. 2, pp. 299-306.

GEORGE, P. (1977), *Memories*, London, The English Centre and the Commonplace Workshop.

GILES, R. (1977), *The West Indian Experience in British Schools*, London, Heinemann.

GLASS, V. (1976), 'Cookery in the Classroom', *Teachers' World*, 2 July.

GOODMAN, K. S. (1965), 'Dialect Barriers to Comprehension', in *Elementary English*, 42, pp. 853-60.

GOODMAN, K. S. (1969), 'Dialect Barriers to Comprehension', in Baratz and Shuy, 1969, pp. 14-28.

GOODMAN, K. S. (1972), 'Reading: a Psycholinguistic Guessing Game', in N. C. Farnes (ed.), *Reading Purposes, Comprehension and the Use of Context*, Milton Keynes, Open University Press, pp. 78-84.

GOODMAN, K. S. and BUCK, C. (1973), 'Dialect Barriers to Reading Comprehension Revisited', *The Reading Teacher*, vol. 27, no. 1, pp. 6-12.

GREGORY, E. (1969), 'Childminding in Paddington', *The Medical Officer*, 5 September.

HALL, S. and JEFFERSON, T. (eds) (1976), *Youth Sub-Cultures in Post-war Britain*, London, Hutchinson.

HAYNES, J. M. (1971), *Educational Assessment of Immigrant Pupils*, Windsor, National Foundation for Educational Research.

HEBDIGE, D. (1976), 'Reggae, Rastas and Rudies', in Hall and Jefferson, 1976, pp. 135-54.

HERBERT, C. (1977), *In the Melting Pot*, London, The English Centre.
HMSO (1977), *Select Committee on Race Relations and Immigration. The West Indian Community Report*.
HERSKOVITS, M. (1937), *Suriname Folk-lore*, Oxford University Press.
HILL, D. (1976), *Teaching in Multiracial Schools*, London, Methuen.
HOBBS, M. (1976), *Teaching in a Multi-Racial Society*, London, Association of Christian Teachers.
HOOD, C., OPPÉ, T. E., PLESS, I. B. and APTE, E. (1970), *Children of West Indian Immigrants – A Study of One Year Olds in Paddington*, London, Institute of Race Relations.
HUNTLEY, A. (1977), *At School Today*, London, Bogle l'Ouverture.
HYMES, D. (ed.) (1971), *Pidginization and Creolization*, Cambridge University Press.
JEFFCOATE, R. (1975), 'Curriculum Planning in Multiracial Education', *Educational Research*, vol. 18, no. 2, pp. 192-200.
JEFFCOATE, R. (1977), 'Schools and Racism', *Multiracial School*, vol. 6, no. 1, pp. 16-24.
JEFFCOATE, R. *et al.* (1978), 'Race and teachers: the Schools Council study', *New Society*, 16 February, pp. 366-8.
JEKYLL, W. (ed.) (1966), *Jamaican Song and Story*, New York, Dover Publications.
JOHN, G. (1972), 'Commentary' in D. Humphrey, *Police Power and Black People*, St Albans, Panther.
JOHNSON, J. (1978b), 'Park Bench Blues', *Race Today*, January, pp. 11-12.
JOHNSON, J. (1978a), 'Ballad For You', *Race Today*, January, pp. 10-11.
JOHNSON, L. K. (1974), 'Voices of the Living and the Dead', *Race Today*, March.
JOHNSON, L. K. (1975), *Dread Beat and Blood*, London, Bogle l'Ouverture.
JOHNSON, L. K. (1976), 'The Reggae Rebellion', *New Society*, 36, 714, p. 589.
KELLER, S. (1963), 'The Social World of the Urban Slum Child: Some Early Findings', *American Journal of Orthopsychiatry*, vol. 33, pp. 823-31.
KIEV, A. (1964), 'Psychotherapeutic Aspects of Pentecostal Sects among West Indian Immigrants to England', *British Journal of Sociology*, vol. XV, no. 2.
KOLERS, P. A. (1973), 'Three Stages in Reading', in Smith, 1973, pp. 28-49.
LABOV, W. (1966), *Social Stratification of English in New York City*, Washington D.C., Center for Applied Linguistics.

LABOV, W. (1969), 'Some Sources of Reading Problems for Negro Speakers of Non-Standard English', in Baratz and Shuy, 1969, pp. 29-67.

LABOV, W. (1972a), 'The Logic of Non-Standard English', in P. P. Giglioli (ed.), *Language and Social Context*, Harmondsworth, Penguin.

LABOV, W. (ed.) (1972b), *Language in the Inner City*, University of Pennsylvania Press.

LABOV, W. and ROBINS, C. (1972), 'A Note on the Relation of Reading Failure to Peer Group Status in Urban Ghettos', in Labov, 1972b, pp. 241-54.

LAMBERT, W. E., HODGSON, R. C., GARDENER, R. C. and FILLENBAUM, S. (1960), 'Evaluational Reactions to Spoken Languages', *Journal of Abnormal and Social Psychology*, vol. 60, pp. 44-51.

LAMMING, G. (1960), *Season of Adventure*, London, Michael Joseph.

LE PAGE, R. B. (1974), 'Processes of Pidginization and Creolization', *York Papers in Linguistics*, vol. 4, pp. 41-69.

LITTLE, A. (1975), 'Educational Achievement of Ethnic Minority Children in London', in Verma and Bagley, 1975, pp. 48-69.

LIU, S. (1976), 'An Investigation of Oral Reading Miscues made by Non-standard Dialect Speaking Black Children', *Reading Research Quarterly*, vol. XI, no. 2, pp. 193-7.

LOUDEN, D. (1977), 'Conflict and Change among West Indian Parents in Britain', *Educational Research*, vol. 20, no. 1, pp. 44-53.

LOWENTHAL, D. (1972), *West Indian Societies*, Oxford University Press.

LOZELLS SOCIAL DEVELOPMENT CENTRE (1975), *Wednesday's Child. A Report on under fives provision in Handsworth*, London, Community Relations Commission.

MARK, Y. *et al.* (1977), *Stepping Out*, London, The Commonplace Workshop.

MILNER, D. (1975), *Children and Race*, Harmondsworth, Penguin.

MORDECAI, J. (1966), 'West Indian Children's Language Study', Dissertation, School of Education, University of Birmingham.

NAIPAUL, V. S. (1961), *A House for Mr Biswas*, London, André Deutsch.

NAIPAUL, V. S. (1967), *A Flag on the Island*, London, André Deutsch.

PEACH, C. (1978), *West Indian Migration to Britain: a social geography*, Oxford University Press.

PIDGEON, W. (1970), *Teacher Expectation and Pupil Performance*, Windsor, National Foundation for Educational Research.

POLLACK, M. (1972a), 'A Suggested Black Studies Syllabus', *Teachers Against Racism*, June.

POLLACK, M. (1972b), *Today's Three Year Olds in London*, London, Heinemann.

ROSE, E. J. *et al.* (1969), *Colour and Citizenship*, Oxford University Press/Institute of Race Relations.

ROSENTHAL, R. and JAKOBSON, L. (1968), *Pygmalion in the Classroom: Teacher Expectation and Pupils' Intellectual Development*, New York, Holt, Rinehart & Winston.

SALKEY, A. (1969), *The Adventures of Catullus Kelly*, London, Hutchinson.

SCHOOLS COUNCIL (1972), *Teaching English to West Indian Children, Concept 7-9*, London, Edward Arnold.

SELIGMAN, C. B., TUCKER, G. R. and LAMBERT, W. E. (1972), 'The Effects of Speech Style and Other Attributes on Teachers' Attitudes towards Pupils', *Language in Society*, vol. 1, pp. 131-42.

SELVON, S. (1963), *I Hear Thunder*, St Albans, MacGibbon & Kee.

SELVON, S. (1965), *The Housing Lark*, St Albans, MacGibbon & Kee.

SELVON, S. (1972), *The Lonely Londoners*, Harlow, Longman.

SELVON, S. (1973), *Ways of Sunlight*, Harlow, Longman.

SHUY, R. (1970), 'Subjective Judgements in Sociolinguistic Analysis', in J. Alatis (ed.), *20th Annual Round Table Meeting on Linguistics and Language Studies*, Georgetown University Press.

SHUY, R. W. (1975), 'Pragmatics: Still Another Contribution of Linguistics to Reading', in S. S. Smiley and J. C. Towner (eds), *Language and Reading, 6th Western Symposium on Learning*, Georgetown University Press.

SMITH, D. (1976), *The Facts of Racial Disadvantage*, London, Political and Economic Planning.

SMITH, D. (1977), *Racial Disadvantage in Britain*, Harmondsworth, Penguin.

SMITH, F. (1971), *Understanding Reading: A Psycholinguistic Analysis of Reading and Learning to Read*, New York, Holt, Rinehart & Winston.

SMITH, F. (1973), *Psycholinguistics and Reading*, New York, Holt, Rinehart & Winston.

SMOLINS, G. (1974), 'Reading and Comprehension: a Comparative Study of some 8-9 year old Children of English and West Indian Origin', M.A. dissertation, Birkbeck College, University of London.

SNOW, R. (1969), 'Review of "Pygmalion in the Classroom" by Rosenthal and Jakobson', *Contemporary Psychology*, vol. 41, pp. 197-9.

STERN, V. and WALLIS, S. (1977), *Caring for Under-Fives in a Multi-Racial Society*, London, Community Relations Commission.

STORM, M. (1971), 'Studies of Distant Environments in Primary Schools: Some Problems', *Teachers' World*, Summer 1971.

STOTT, D. H. (1971), *The Social Adjustment of Children, Bristol Social Adjustment Guides Manual*, University of London Press, 4th edn.

SUTCLIFFE, D. (1976), 'Hou dem Taak in Bedford, Sa', *Multiracial School*, vol. 5, no. 1, pp. 19-24.

SUTCLIFFE, D. (1978), 'The Language of First and Second Generation West Indian Children in Bedfordshire', M.Ed. thesis, University of Leicester.

THORNDIKE, R. L. (1968), 'Review of Rosenthal and Jakobson, "Pygmalion in the Classroom"', *American Educational Research Journal*, vol, 5, no. 4, pp. 708-11.

TORREY, J. (1973), 'Illiteracy in the Ghetto', in Smith, 1973, pp. 131-7.

TOUGH, J. (1976), *The Development of Meaning: a Study of Children's Use of Language*, London, Allen & Unwin.

TOWNSEND, H. E. R. (1971), *Immigrant Pupils in England: the L.E.A. Response*, Windsor, National Foundation for Educational Research.

TOWNSEND, H. E. R. and BRITTAN, E. M. (1972), *Organisation in Multiracial Schools*, Windsor, National Foundation for Educational Research.

TOWNSEND, H. E. R. and BRITTAN, E. M. (1973), *Multiracial Education, Need and Innovation: The Preliminary Report of the Schools Council Education for a Multiracial Society Project*, London, Evans.

TROYNA, B. (1977a), 'The Reggae War', *New Society*, Vol. 39, pp. 490-1.

TROYNA, B. (1977b), 'Angry Youngsters – a Response to Racism in Britain', *Youth in Society*, no. 26, December, pp. 13-15.

TROYNA, B. (1977c), 'The Rastafarians – The Youth's Response', *Multiracial School*, vol. 6, no. 1, pp. 1-8.

TROYNA, B. (1978), 'Race and Streaming'; a case study, *Educational Review*, vol. 30, no. 1.

TRUDGILL, P. (1975), *Accent, Dialect and the School*, London, Edward Arnold.

TRUDGILL, P. and GILES, H. (forthcoming), 'Sociolinguistic and Linguistic Value Judgements: Correctness, Adequacy and Aesthetics', in *The Functionality of Language*, Ghent, Belgium, Story Scientia.

VERMA, G. K. and BAGLEY, C. (1975), *Race and Education Across Cultures*, London, Heinemann.

WIGHT, J. (1976), 'How Much Interference?' *Times Educational Supplement*, 14 May.

WIGHT, J., HUNT, P., SAPARA, S. and SINCLAIR, H. (1978a), *Explore-A-Story*, London, Collins in collaboration with ILEA's Learning Materials Service.

WIGHT, J., HUNT, P., SAPARA, S. and SINCLAIR, H. (1978b), *Share-A-Story*, Edinburgh, Holmes McDougall in collaboration with ILEA's Learning Materials Service.

WIGHT, J., HUNT, P., SAPARA, S. and SINCLAIR, H. (1978c), *Make-A-Story*, ILEA's Learning Materials Service.

WIGHT, J. and NORRIS, R. (1970), *Teaching English to West Indian Children: The Research Stage of the Project*, Schools Council Working Paper 29, London, Evans/Methuen Educational.

WILLIAMS, F. (1973), 'Some Research Notes on Dialect Attitudes and Stereotypes', in Shuy, R. and Fasold, R. (eds), *Language Attitudes: Current Trends and Prospects*, Georgetown University Press, pp. 113-28.

WILLIAMS, F., WHITEHEAD, J. L. and MILLER, L. M. (1971), 'Ethnic Stereotyping and Judgements of Children's Speech', *Speech Monographs*, vol. 38, pp. 166-70.

WILLSHER, S., CALLAGHAN, B. *et al.* (1977), 'A Multiracial High School Speaks', *Multiracial School*, Spring.

WOLFRAM, W. (1969), *A Sociolinguistic Description of Detroit Negro Speech*, Washington D.C., Center for Applied Linguistics.

WORRALL, M. (1976), 'Curriculum Strategies for Multiracial Education', *Multiracial School*, vol. 4, no. 3, pp. 17-28.

YOUNG, C. N. (1973), 'Belize Creole: A Study of the Creolized English Spoken in the City of Belize in its Cultural and Social Setting', Unpublished D.Phil. thesis, University of York.

Index